# BRIGHT NOTES

# MAJOR BARBARA BY GEORGE BERNARD SHAW

**Intelligent Education**

Nashville, Tennessee

BRIGHT NOTES: Major Barbara
www.BrightNotes.com

No part of this publication may be used or reproduced in any manner whatsoever without written permission, except in the case of brief quotations in critical articles and reviews. For permissions, contact Influence Publishers http://www.influencepublishers.com.

ISBN: 978-1-645421-54-2 (Paperback)
ISBN: 978-1-645421-55-9 (eBook)

Published in accordance with the U.S. Copyright Office Orphan Works and Mass Digitization report of the register of copyrights, June 2015.

Originally published by Monarch Press.
Joan Thellusson Nourse, 1965
2019 Edition published by Influence Publishers.

Interior design by Lapiz Digital Services. Cover Design by Thinkpen Designs.

Printed in the United States of America.

Library of Congress Cataloging-in-Publication Data forthcoming.
Names: Intelligent Education
Title: BRIGHT NOTES: Major Barbara
Subject: STU004000 STUDY AIDS / Book Notes

# CONTENTS

| | | |
|---|---|---|
| 1) | Introduction to Major Barbara | 1 |
| 2) | The Preface | 15 |
| 3) | Textual Analysis | |
| | Act 1, Scenes 1 and 2 | 22 |
| | Act 1, Scenes 3 and 4; Act 2, Scene 1 | 39 |
| | Act 2, Scenes 2 - 4 | 55 |
| | Act 2, Scenes 5 - 7 | 70 |
| | Act 2, Scene 8; Act 3, Scene 1 | 107 |
| | Act 3, Scenes 2 and 3 | 126 |
| 9) | Analyses Of Major Characters | 142 |
| 10) | Essay Questions And Answers | 148 |

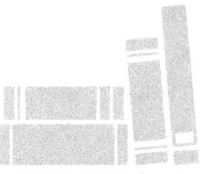

# MAJOR BARBARA

## INTRODUCTION

### GRAND OPENING

In the late autumn of 1905 London theatergoers were happily agog over the prospects of a new comedy by George Bernard Shaw called *Major Barbara*. Rumors had indicated that it was to be about the Salvation Army, surely an unusual **theme** for drawing-room repartee. But then that witty, red-bearded Irish playwright, with the bold Socialist leanings, had proved that he could fashion amusing, provocative plays out of the most unlikely material. During the thirteen years since his first play, *Widowers' Houses*, had commanded their attention, they had applauded such entertaining pieces as *Candida,* The *Devil's Disciple*, *Caesar and Cleopatra*, and *Man and Superman.* So they eagerly awaited his latest offering, their curiosity further titillated by the hint of possible censorship problems over a Biblical quotation.

On November 28th, the first performance took place in the afternoon before a glittering audience of notables, including the Prime Minister himself, Arthur James Balfour. The Conservative leader's coming was quite a compliment to Shaw, for a national election was impending, and even his own party was seriously divided over imperialism, tariffs, and the rights of trade unions. And the recent conclusions of the Russo-Japanese War had by no means solved all problems in the Far East. But to miss the opening at the Royal Court Theatre would be unthinkable for a statesman with any interest in the cultural scene. The intelligentsia was there in force. Even more starting to some, however, was the presence in box seats to several Salvation Army Commissioners, in uniform. For it was known that many strict Methodist members of this organization regarded the stage as a moral hazard.

## THE FIRST PRODUCTION

The acting company was under the direction of J. E. Vedrenne, a skilled theatrical entrepreneur, and Harley Granville-Barker, known as an actor, a producer, and later as a leading Shakespearean critic. In *Major Barbara* Granville-Barker played the role of Adolphus Cusins, the young professor of Greek, who loves the heroine, Barbara. He is said to have handled perceptively this complex character which Shaw based upon that of his admired friend, Gilbert Murray, a famous classical scholar.

For Andrew Undershaft, the keen-minded, strong-willed munitions magnate who expresses some of Shaw's most controversial views, the choice was Louis Calvert, a solidly built, experienced Shakespearean actor with the requisite imposing manner. He seemed an ideal selection, having already won approval as Broadbent, the oracular businessman in Shaw's *John Bull's Other Island*. Yet his new portrayal proved disappointing. As he later ruefully admitted, he simply did not understand at the time the inner workings of the role. Subsequently, when he repeated the part in New York, he apparently gained insight. But

Undershaft is probably the play's pivotal character. And Calvert's uncertainty undoubtedly tended to decrease the work's initial dramatic impact.

According to Shaw, however, all were enthusiastic about the winsome and spirited young actress, Annie Russell, who played Barbara, the Earl's granddaughter who joins the Salvation Army to bring a new vision to the poor and the lost. Originally, the playwright had hoped to engage the lovely American Eleanor Robson, later known to society here as Mrs. August Belmont. But the Robson demands were too high, and her friend, Miss Russell, proved a captivating substitute.

## CRITICAL REACTION

Like most other dramatists, however well established, Shaw was vitally interested in the reception his play would receive. He was never one, having from boyhood the pinch of an insufficient income, to be careless about financial returns. He could, in fact, drive fairly hard bargains. In addition, he seems to have cared a great deal about the views on religion, education, economics, and social that he was advancing more seriously than ever in this play. So how people reacted was quite important. *Major Barbara* is divided into three acts. After the first two, on that November afternoon, the applause was tumultuous, and Shaw's hopes soared. The last act, he realized, was unusually long and was largely talk rather than action. But "they'll eat it," he assured a skeptical and sympathetic fellow-dramatist.

He was overly optimistic. Some ordinary playgoers grew impatient toward the end, finding the argument on poverty, wealth, and the moral aspects of munitions manufacture confusing and somewhat wearisome. Indeed, even some of the leading theatre critics of the day were alienated by the extended discussions. Arthur Bingham Walkley, a cultivated writer who liked shows to be graceful and amusing, thought the work a bewildering hodge-podge. And William Archer, a close friend of Shaw, was disappointed to find no genuine human beings. Only those who, like Sir Oliver Lodge and William T. Stead, were primarily interested in stimulating ideas reacted with enthusiasm. Most, said Shaw himself, condemned the author for not having written a play at all.

Nevertheless, the work did run at the Court for the maximum possible period of six weeks, even though toward the end few were attending any theatres because of the general election that would end Balfour's tenure. As indicated above, *Major Barbara* later played fairly successfully in the United States, with Calvert and Grace George. Also in this 1915 cast were such other names later famed in the American theatre as Clarence Derwent, Conway Tearle, John Cromwell, and Guthrie McClintic. There followed a screen version in 1940, the script of which has been published.

## LATER CRITICISM

During the more than 50 years since *Major Barbara* opened, the play has received further critical attention, much of it quite favorable. The astute Gilbert K. Chesterton, it is true, regretted its "materialistic pessimism," and Edmund Fuller, its "curiously negative, compromised quality." And the politically oriented have argued heatedly as to its alignment with Marxist or capitalist views. Shaw's biographer, Archibald Henderson, speaking more generally, called it "powerful and impressive," Edward Everett Hale, Jr. considered it "much the best" of the later plays. Probably few would take up the fairly recent challenge of the American critic Joseph Frank to see it possibly as "one of the great works of the twentieth century." But it is interesting to consider another of Mr. Frank's suggestions, namely, that *Major Barbara* is an epitome, or summing up, of much that is characteristically Shavian.

## BRIEF SUMMARY

The first act opens in a well-appointed library in fashionable Wilton Crescent. An assertive dowager, Lady Britomart, has summoned home for a visit her husband, Andrew Undershaft, a millionaire munitions maker. They have long been separated because he has refused to leave his business to Stephen, their son, since an industry tradition insists that he choose as heir a bright, capable foundling. Lady Britomart, though still unappeased, has condescended to ask that he provide their two daughters, now engaged, with handsome supplementary incomes. Sarah, pale and indolent, will marry Charles Lomax, a fatuous youth with good but remote inheritance prospects. Barbara, vital and sensible, has chosen Adolphus Cusins, a brainy but moneyless professor. Arriving on cue, the genial but forceful Undershaft is most impressed with Barbara, who wears the uniform of a major in the Salvation Army. The subject of religion having arisen, he agrees to let her try to convert him at her shelter in the slums, if she will let him show her his munitions works the next day.

Act II, taking place at the bleak West Ham center of the Army, introduces Rummy Mitchens and Snobby Price, ill-fed, poorly clothed Cockneys who sham conversions for free handouts. Also arriving is Peter Shirley, a starving unemployed workman, an ardent Secularist. Then in bursts truculent Bill Walker, demanding that the Army return a former love of his, now reformed. Infuriated when denied, he strikes Jenny Hill, a young Salvationist lass. Coming on the scene, Barbara stirs his conscience, so that he wants to square matters by receiving an equal blow or paying a fine of sorts. But she says that salvation cannot be bought. Her coolly calculating father then demonstrates that he can at least "buy" the Army by having them accept a huge check despite their disapproval of the wars his weapons make so deadly. Horrified, Barbara removes her Army emblem and pins it on Undershaft, as Walker offers taunts. The idealistic Barbara thus is sadly disillusioned, as her father intended.

The last act brings the Undershafts and their friends to Perivale St. Andrews. All are astonished to find the munitions town a marvel of fine houses, clean streets, and well-paid, spirited workers. Undershaft then declares that the worst crime of all is poverty. By providing high wages, he saves more souls than Barbara ever could. Cusins, here fiance, having satisfied the foundling technicality, agrees to be Undershaft's successor, but only to "make war on war." After some hesitation, Barbara decides to transfer her spiritual ministrations to the Undershaft employees, whom she need not "bribe" with bread as she did the starving. She will talk to them of highest and holiest things. The Major thus returns to the colors.

## SHAW AND THE ARMY

During the first years after coming to London from his native Ireland, Shaw became much interested in the Fabian Society and other movements formed to correct social evils. He became a skilled and effective speaker for these groups and often talked to street-corner crowds in the poorer districts. He thus came frequently into contact with Salvation Army missionaries holding their meetings in the same locale. Always musically inclined, Shaw was particularly delighted with the rousing hymns played by their bands.

Years later, after he had achieved a reputation both as a music and drama critic and as a playwright, he was much annoyed when a journalist made a casual slurring reference to Salvation Army music. Springing to the defense of his old acquaintances, Shaw wrote a tribute that won him a grateful invitation to attend the Army's next band festival at Clapham Hall. Continuing the association, Shaw suggested that perhaps the Army might be able to use short plays to interest its potential converts. And he offered technical assistance. Nothing came of the proposal, but Shaw did think more and more of the Army's operations as dramatic material and eventually wrote *Major Barbara*, for which the Army lent uniforms as costumes.

## CHILDHOOD PREPARATION

Yet in some sense the genesis of the work is traceable to Shaw's earliest experiences as a boy in Dublin. He was born on July 26, 1856, the son of George Carr Shaw, an amiable, kindly gentleman with no head for business and a disconcerting fondness for alcohol. His mother, Elizabeth Gurly, an imaginative lady with above-average musical gifts, was notable for her independent thinking, dignified aloofness, vivacity, and good humor. As in *Major Barbara* the family consisted of one boy and two girls.

Culturally, Shaw's home provided good opportunities for a future writer. He had access to books and music, and considerable freedom to develop individual preferences. His parents were agreeable enough but do not seem to have sought any close association with their children. Young Shaw was cared for mostly by servants.

Among his earlier memories were those of walks through the dismal slums of Dublin. Nursemaids instructed to take him to the park slipped off with him instead to visit friends. There the boy became acquainted with the dirt, disease, and drink-induced wretchedness that went with poverty. Later works, notably *Major Barbara*, were to reflect his profound conviction that such deplorable conditions should be corrected.

In addition to his own observations, he read such works as Dickens's *Hard Times*, that spelled out the sad lot of the impoverished. And although he himself seems never to have suffered real penury, he knew as a boy the meaning of financial pressures. His father put all his capital into a corn business that brought him close to ruin. His mother's marriage cost her a large inheritance, and eventually, having left her husband, she was obliged to support herself by giving music lessons. The Shaws were a proud family, but there was never quite enough money to enable them to feel secure.

## RELIGIOUS SENTIMENTS

If his youthful experiences helped to create that horror of poverty so pronounced in *Major Barbara*, there is also evidence that certain attitudes Shaw takes therein toward religion went back to childhood impressions. In *Major Barbara* only the rigidly conventional or frankly foolish characters belong to the Established Church. Barbara is a Salvation Army evangelist, and her father has made up his own creed. His religion, he says, is that of a Millionaire, with its principal commandment, forbidding its votaries ever to be poor. And Cusins, the classics professor, merely claims to be a "collector of religions," who somehow believes in them all.

The Shaws were Protestants in largely Catholic Dublin. The playwright's father sometimes talked of the Bible with sardonic humor, suggesting a skeptical attitude. And his mother seemed diffident about imposing any firm beliefs upon the children. There were family prayers for a time, as well as Sunday school and compulsory attendance at bleak services. And some of the Catholic maids added their incidental instruction. But the boy fairly early rejected orthodoxy, and Shaw later associated in London with many who were free thinkers.

He seems, however, to consider himself a "religious" man and to regard all serious individuals as also being so. From the evolutionists and other modern thinkers, he took over and developed a concept of a Life-Force-operating through matter and therefore through men-that was forever seeking higher levels. The good or religious individual was therefore one who rose above petty personal concerns and consciously exercised his full capabilities to make himself and others better, happier, nobler. Shaw talks often of God. But God to him, according to C. E. M. Joad, may mean simply "the principle of change and development in the universe." Undershaft does the work of the Life-Force by lifting himself out of dire poverty and becoming rich and powerful. He also saves his workers from the deadening effects of poverty and so enlightens his daughter that she can make an even better use of her own superior talents. Barbara, on her part, also labors to bring the poor and ignorant a new sense of their dignity as people, and Cusins hopes, by warring upon war, to make a better existence possible for thousands. Chesterton, for one, regarded Shaw's religious views rather critically. How could anyone, he inquired wittily, worship a hyphen? But Shaw, although he could never boast about converts, apparently found his synthesis satisfactory. And it is worth noting that whereas he disliked some traditional Christian doctrines, such as that of the Atonement, he could give qualified approval to a group such as the Salvation Army insofar as their workers helped the deprived to raise their sights.

## LONDON AND SOCIALISM

Having completed a desultory formal education and having worked for a brief period for an Irish estate agent, Shaw came to seek his fortune in London in 1876, at the age of twenty. During the next few years, he wrote *Immaturity* and several other novels, grew a quite impressive-looking beard, and became a dedicated vegetarian. Then in 1882 he attended a lecture by Henry George, an American who questioned why landholders should get the exclusive benefits from property whose value they had done nothing to increase. Fascinated by the speaker's views, Shaw began to read up on socialism and other movements demanding changes in the capitalist system. He read, among other works, the writings of Karl Marx, but later became associated with the Fabian Society, which tended to seek more gradual improvements than did the Marxists.

By the time *Major Barbara* was written, Shaw was no longer so actively engaged in lecturing and writing on Socialism, Fabian or otherwise. He had, however, been profoundly affected by his former associations, and kept up friendships with those who had been similarly active. In this play, his hero in an unashamed capitalist, and there is no question of state controls such as would be required for a socialistic system. In the Preface the idea is advanced that all should receive a fair share of money and that the able-bodied should all be compelled to work. But Undershaft in effect announces that he is the state, and government interference with him is not apparent.

The only explanation suggested is that Undershaft probably represents a transitional stage. He feeds and clothes the workers and educates them to secure his own best interest. But the workers growing stronger physically and otherwise will eventually demand more and more of a share until the Socialistic millenium of economic equality is achieved. Lest, however, this seem too slow, Cusins is talking mysteriously of helping the common people by handing them direct power, perhaps guns. This suggests the possibility of more violent action, and Undershaft himself insists that if something is worth attaining it may be worth shedding blood. Shaw, in general, is known as a gradualist. So presumably he would prefer the orderly changeover suggested in the Undershaft plan.

## MARRIAGE AND LATER LIFE

In 1898, six years before writing *Major Barbara*, Shaw married Charlotte Payne-Townshend, a wealthy woman who shared his intellectual interests. Neither was under forty, and there was no suggestion of intense romantic passion. But the two seem to have shared an agreeable life together until her death in 1943 at the age of 86. Shaw also is known to have carried on flirtatious correspondences with such noted actresses as Ellen Terry and Mrs. Patrick Campbell, but again the stress was always upon the sharing of ideas. Lady Britomart in his play discourages affectionate nonsense. And while Adolphus and Barbara snatch a kiss over his big Salvation Army drum, both insist that other claims must take precedence over their love affair.

In 1905, the year in which *Major Barbara* opened, the Shaws bought the house at Ayot St. Lawrence, in a pleasant Hertfordshire village. In later years this unpretentious country home became a place of pilgrimage for many notables. Shaw, of course, went on writing plays. *The Doctor's Dilemma, Pygmalion,* and *St. Joan* were among his later works. And in 1925 he was awarded the Nobel Prize. Toward the end of his life he antagonized some by his rather uncritical approval of foreign dictatorships. But he was mourned as a respected man of letters when he died at 94 in 1950.

## SHAW AS PLAYWRIGHT

Although Shaw was unwilling to acknowledge much influence from contemporary playwrights, he was from the first linked to some extent with Henrik Ibsen. Like Ibsen, his tone was realistic. He dealt with contemporary social problems. He had a reforming spirit. And at times he utilized some of the tight construction of the Ibsen "well-made play." The events in *Major Barbara*, for instance, take place within a very few days, and the blood and fire symbolism is used to advantage. On the other hand, some feel that he differs greatly from Ibsen in that he is much more witty and amusing.

Both Ibsen, and Norwegian playwright, and Strindberg, the Swedish one, pictured the "new woman," a type quite removed from the more empty-headed romantic heroines. She was more independent, more aggressive, sometimes more dangerous, generally more interesting. Shaw again claims that his ideas were derived from native thinkers and his own observations. But Barbara, although by no means so disagreeable as some of her overseas sisters, has certainly their force, directness, and determination.

## OUTSTANDING QUALITIES

In general, then, Shaw is noted for clever, intellectual comedies often expressing controversial ideas. He criticizes contemporary religion and morality. He talks of socialism and other systems. He has comments and opinions on almost all contemporary questions, and delights in **irony** and paradox.

As for his characters, they are first of all surprising. The unscrupulous industrialist may turn out to be an admirable figure. The attractive young man may be proved a fool or weakling. There are, however, certain types that seem to appear with some regularity. There is the cool, brainy, superman hero, typified by Undershaft. There is the bright, determined girl represented by Barbara. And there is the outspoken uneducated individual, such as Bill Walker of Doolittle, the dustman in *Pygmalion*.

The plots are not his main concern, and there are long sections in which discussion is paramount. But he can write powerful scenes. Here the disillusioning of Barbara is always an effective **episode**. And some of the intellectual duels are exciting anyway.

## OVER-ALL EVALUATION

Even today there is no clear agreement as to Shaw's permanent standing. Some find him too much the showman, other too little. There are those who point out that he shrewdly anticipated certain modern developments along socialistic lines. And there are other who find his Life-Force theories absurd and his most shocking notions merely dated. Finally, there are those who do not seem to care exactly what he said but are interested in the artistic effects he achieved while saying it.

In any event his plays still draw audiences. Within the last quarter of a century, Americans, for instance, have seen many noted performers assay his roles. Katherine Cornell and Maurice Evans, Charles Laughton and Siobhan McKenna, Katherine Hepburn and Robert Preston are but a few of the stars who have appeared. And, as all will recall, his *Pygmalion* provided the basis for the great musical show and award-winning film, *My Fair Lady*.

Apart from the obvious appeal of musical adaptations, the Shaw comedies seem to amuse most those who, being tired of the inane conventional chatter in many of today's works, seek out some literate, clever dialogue and a few ideas scintillatingly discussed. Probably few leave with any strong urge to emulate Undershaft, and less with any call to start evangelizing a large aircraft plant. But they enjoy watching Undershaft, Cusins, and Barbara forge their destinies, welcoming for a change some able, intelligent forthright characters with daring visions to pursue.

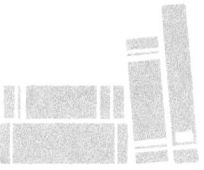

# MAJOR BARBARA

## THE PREFACE

### GENERAL INTRODUCTION

Shaw accompanies many of his published plays with prefaces that include detailed discussion of points covered in the dialogue. The one for *Major Barbara* runs about forty pages, and deals with the views of Undershaft on wealth, the efforts of Barbara to awaken Walker's conscience, and other matters such as Shaw's literary sources and his opinions about such legal penalties as fines and imprisonment. In the course of the long essay there are many **allusions** to a variety of authors, ancient and modern. Shaw refers to such foreign writers as Ibsen and Tolstoy and such British novelists as Dickens and Charles Lever. He mentions some of his associates from the early days when he gave talks for the Fabians, and he brings in comparisons from masterpieces by Cervantes, Froissart, and Shakespeare.

### CRITICAL ATTITUDES

Basically there are three different views expressed by critics about such prefaces. First, there are those who think that Shaw should be content to let his play speak for itself. If he is clear and intelligible therein, they argue, why is there need for so much additional explanation?

The second contingent suggests that Shaw was always more the polemicist or propagandist than the playwright. They are of the opinion that in the preface one finds the real Shaw, unhampered by the fettering restrictions of stage conventions. They would almost be willing to skip the plays (as being mere oversimplified restatements to please the less mature) and concentrate on the fuller discussions.

The third group, generally today in the majority, regard play and prefaces as supplementary. They feel that on the whole the dramas are strong enough to succeed on their own merits, but they welcome the further enlightenment which the prefaces provide as to Shaw's basic thinking. This is an age of research and most scholars are glad to peruse carefully any pieces of writing that give more information as to the sources of a work or that merely reveal a little more about the mind behind the masterpiece.

## Note

The preface is divided into several sections:

## FIRST AID TO CRITICS

In this opening part, Shaw takes issue with those who seek the origin of his views in readings from such foreign writers as Nietzsche and Ibsen. Shaw claims instead that he was influenced much more by such native authors as the lesser-known Charles Lever and by such acquaintances of his from Fabian and other groups as Wilson, Belfort Bax, and Stuart-Glennie.

## THE GOSPEL OF ST. ANDREW UNDERSHAFT

In this part, he defends Undershaft's position that the greatest of all evils is poverty. Shaw examines in detail the attendant woes and also takes a strong position as regards the injustice of imprisoning malefactors. Two wrongs do not make a right, and imprisonment is a cruel torture. He suggests that poverty should be legally outlawed. Everyone might be given enough to live on well and then be expected to earn it by useful work. He does not go deeply into the matter of how such an arrangement could be achieved without any intolerable forcing of the individual.

## THE SALVATION ARMY

He discusses amusedly the confusion of critics as to whether or not he was attacking the Army. The Army understood perfectly, he insists, how necessary it was for Mrs. Baines to take the money.

## BARBARA'S RETURN TO THE COLORS

Barbara has to learn that there are disadvantages to preaching a salvation that must partially base its appeal upon the bribe of bread and treacle. But there is something about the joyous and militant spirit of the Army that Shaw finds admirable.

## WEAKNESSES OF THE SALVATION ARMY

Shaw dislikes the Army's insistence upon confession and distrusts any religious system that emphasizes a system of atonement that may encourage offenders to feel justified once more and so free to sin again. Barbara, on the contrary, really opens Bill's eyes, while she has the chance, as to the true nature of his offense. He will thus be less likely to commit it again. The Army should further urge the poor to go after their rights, not preach submission, thus acting as a tool of the rich.

## CHRISTIANITY AND ANARCHISM

Referring to a recent international incident in which demands were made for the cruel punishment of some rebels, Shaw charges that Christianity is not true to its principles. It should be cheering those who seek a better life, not insisting that they be butchered.

## SANE CONCLUSIONS

Summing up his position, he recommends that all the able-bodied be expected to work. He also would rule out harsh punishments. An offender should be warned and tolerated, but, upon persisting, killed. He further stresses again that there should be no talk of atonement-wrongdoing should be seen as irrevocable. Finally, he urges all creeds to become intellectually honest.

### Comment

Most of the basic ideas in the preface are clearly stated in the play. The exceptions are as follows: the stress upon equalization of income and compulsory labor, the detailed discussion of his views on crime and punishment, and the information as to his sources. Shaw, incidentally, is almost always loath to admit the influence of foreign authors.

## CHARACTERS

### Stephen Undershaft

A stiffly proper young English gentleman in his twenties, devoid of interest in, or talent for, any profession, but positive that he can distinguish between right and wrong.

### Lady Britomart Undershaft

An autocratic matriarch of about fifty and the daughter of an Earl, who cannot tolerate her husband's unconventional views and wants above all to secure the Undershaft inheritance for her unpromising son.

### Barbara Undershaft

A cheerful, energetic, idealistic young woman willing to work hard at her Salvation Army shelter to bring salvation to the poor.

### Sarah Undershaft

Her languid, slightly bored sister, who can yet on occasion betray surprising hints of acumen and courage.

### Andrew Undershaft

A cool-headed, resolute munitions magnate, who appears easy-going and genial, but has no qualms about using unorthodox means to achieve his goals.

### Jenny Hill

A pale, sweet, kindly Salvationist lass, at times close to hysteria.

### Bill Walker

A rude, truculent young Cockney, who can yet be prodded into feeling remorse for blows struck in anger.

### Morrison

The Undershaft butler, an old retainer, somewhat confused as to how the Master should be received when visiting the family he supports.

### Adolphus Cusins

A quick-thinking, amiable professor of Greek, engaged to Barbara and quite interested in Undershaft's ideas and Undershaft's need for a successor.

### Charles Lomax

A silly, vapid young prospective millionaire, engaged to Sarah and much better at playing the concertina than he is at expressing profundities.

### Rummy Mitchens

An ill-fed, poorly clad woman at the shelter who denies her respectability because the lasses pay more heed to sinners with lurid pasts.

### Snobby Price

Another fake convert, a boastful but lazy fellow, who confesses he had beaten his mother but flees terrified whenever she comes after him.

### Peter Shirley

An older, unemployed factory worker who as an ardent Secularist and anti-capitalist feels smugly superior morally to those with money.

### Bilton

A respectful but uncowed Undershaft employee who will not let the gentry take matches into munitions sheds.

### Mrs. Baines

A harassed but hopeful Salvation Army Commissioner using whatever arguments prove effective to talk rich men out of whatever funds she needs to keep her shelters open.

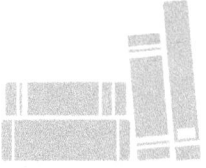

# MAJOR BARBARA

## TEXTUAL ANALYSIS

## ACT 1, SCENES 1 AND 2

### ACT I, SCENE 1

#### SUMMARY

On a January evening, in 1906, Lady Britomart Undershaft has summoned her son Stephen for a conference in the library of their well-appointed London home. A formidable matriarch in her fifties, she alarms that proper, docile youth by insisting that at twenty-four he must now act as responsible family advisor. Actually, of course, she will tolerate only advice that ratifies her prior decisions. He knows, she declares, that his sisters, Barbara and Sarah, are engaged to gentlemen of limited means and will thus need sizable incomes of their own after marriage. So she has arranged a visit tonight from her estranged husband, Andrew, a multimillionaire. Stephen is stunned and angry, for he disapproves of his father's trade of munitions making.

Yet like his mother he, too, resents Undershaft's intent to leave the business not to him but to a foundling, in accord with an industry tradition. Stephen would proudly refuse all funds, but the practical Lady Britomart notes that they have all lived on munitions money for years. Defeated, the young man "advises" her to proceed with her plan. She is pleased with his good sense.

## Comment

Like the opening scenes of most plays, this is mainly devoted to **exposition**, providing us with information about the characters and their interests so that we may be able to follow the action of the play. This expository function of the scene may be considered under three headings:

## UPPER-CLASS SETTING

The library itself with its tasteful dark leather settee and generally impeccable furnishings would immediately suggest that the characters will be people of wealth and position. This impression will be furthered by the fine clothes, dignified bearing, and cultivated speech of Lady Britomart and her son. In addition, several other items establish their social and economic standing. First of all, Lady Britomart makes quite a point of the fact that she is the daughter of the Earl of Stevenage, who would be a man of fairly high rank in the British peerage. Second, Stephen has attended Harrow, one of the better private preparatory schools, and Cambridge University. He has also completed his education, as a young gentleman of the time would, by traveling abroad to India and

Japan. Third, the family is used to servants. Barbara dismissed her personal maid upon joining the Salvation Army, and as the scene ends, Morrison the butler will respond to her Ladyship's ring. Fourth, there are the marriage prospects of the girls. Lady Britomart has arranged a match between Sarah and Charles Lomax, who will one day inherit a million. Meanwhile she insists that both girls must have individual incomes to enable them to run town houses of their own. She wants, for instance, 2,000 pounds annually for Barbara. In the early 1900s, this would equal at least $10,000, with considerably greater purchasing power than the amount would represent today. Finally there are several introductory references to the power and scope of Andrew Undershaft's vast munitions-making business. Hostile schoolmates often taunted Stephen about his father's dealing in destruction, whereas the more wealth-conscious boys fawned on him because of the Undershaft millions. Lady Britomart herself refers to her husband as "rolling in money," or "fabulously wealthy."

The pronounced emphasis upon gracious living and high finance serves several purposes. In the first place, it suggests disarmingly that this will be another lively, pleasant show in the tradition of English drawing-room comedy. Earlier comedies by William Congreve, Richard Brinsley Sheridan, and Oliver Goldsmith, for instance, had all dealt with people of means and leisure. And almost every such play had one or two young couples in love who had some problem of future financial support. Moreover, the domineering but amusing mother, represented by Lady Britomart, would also seem in keeping with the type of light satiric pieces that had produced Sheridan's word-mangling Mrs. Malaprop and Goldsmith's possessive mother, Mrs. Hardcastle. Actually, Shaw is not going to be much concerned at all about the girls' income after marriage, nor will Lady Britomart and Stephen figure prominently in the play's development. Furthermore, the scene will soon shift from drawing-room territory to a Salvation Army shelter in the slums and to a great munitions factory. But Shaw first attracts his audience's interest by providing them with a few familiar elements from standard romantic comedies.

Secondly, this impeccably upper-class setting will make possible some striking dramatic contrasts. Both the library itself and the two staunchly respectable characters will make the upcoming West Ham scene with its wretched, whining, conniving Cockneys and overworked missionaries seem all the more a world apart. And, on the other hand, the formidable figure of Andrew Undershaft, multimillionaire munitions czar, with far-reaching power in political and economic circles, will show up more impressively against the solid but extremely limited library realm of his wife and son. Shaw himself describes Lady Britomart as picturing the universe in terms of her "large house in Wilton Crescent." And the playwright clearly wants us to recognize quickly the limitations of her universe by extending our own intellectual horizons.

Finally, the setting is going to be made in a subtle way a part of Shaw's varied arguments against the more conservative elements in English life. As the play develops, Undershaft will try to convince the idealistic Barbara that she should view poverty as a crime and appreciate the good life made possible by munitions profits. The comfortable home of Lady Britomart and Barbara is visual support in advance for this reasoning. On the other hand, Undershaft's other daring speculations and theories will perhaps receive a better hearing when contrasted with the inane platitudes of such drawing-room types as Lady Britomart, Stephen, Sarah, and Charles Lomax, her fiance.

## CHARACTERS

Although this opening scene shows us primarily the autocratic upper-class matron and her son, it supplies brief and illuminating notes about the other characters.

## LADY BRITOMART

Clearly dominating the scene as she does her grown son, this doughty daughter of the Earl of Stevenage is used to giving peremptory orders. At the very outset she treats the twenty-four-year-old Stephen like a pre-school tot. He must not fidget or fool with tie or watch chain, and, above all, he must not interrupt. Such exhortations, of course, provide good comic possibilities. The managerial woman and the meek, harassed man are usually a combination incongruous enough to excite laughter. And Shaw cannily points up the humor by having this fearsome female blandly aver that she is "only a woman," in need of her educated offspring's "advice," a pronouncement that seems as preposterous to the audience as it does to Stephen. Two other amusing aspects, however, may be noted.

First of all, the lady's name "Britomart" might well recall to those familiar with the works of the English poet Edmund Spenser a leading character from the latter's **epic** work *The Faerie Queene*. In that poem Britomart was a powerful female knight, symbolizing militant chastity. And in any event, the combination of "British" and "martial" in the name would certainly serve Shaw's turn. In addition, however, the character in general is said to have been based upon the historical figure of Lady Carlisle, imperious mother-in-law of Shaw's friend, Gilbert Murray, the Greek scholar said to be the original for Barbara's fiance, Adolphus Cusins. It is thus quite possible that those theatergoers who were acquainted with Shaw and his circle may well have enjoyed a few extra chuckles in recognizing the character's source.

In addition to her comic role, however, Lady Britomart also represents a certain type of Shavian woman, seen usually as a powerful antagonist to a man of unusual talents. According to Shaw's philosophy of the Life Force, the creative man must be free if he is to use his talents to improve civilization in general. Woman, however, contributes to the advancement of life mainly by having children. She therefore sees in a man a potential husband and father and discourages any attempt on his part to be daring or original and thus jeopardize her children's support. She stands, according to the critic C. E. M. Joad, for "security, conservatism, **realism** and common sense" (Shaw, p. 187). Lady Britomart's conservatism is apparent throughout. She clearly deplores her husband's unconventional thinking. But, more important, she has separated from him because he proposed to leave the business to someone other than their son Stephen. She obviously gave Undershaft an ultimatum - either yield to her about Stephen or be denied her presence. This is a strong-minded woman used to getting what she wants. The fact that Undershaft was able to hold out without losing his genial or generous good nature should identify him as one of Shaw's truly superior men, comparable to Caesar in his *Caesar and Cleopatra*. The latter, for instance, never allows the fascinating Egyptian queen to interfere at all with his serious plans.

Finally, Lady Britomart is both shrewd and practical. Regardless of her attitudes toward various characters, she provides a fairly reliable analysis of their personalities, and thus serves admirably her function of providing much of the play's initial **exposition**. She may consider the prospective millionaire, Charles Lomax, a good match for Sarah, but she does not contend that he is witty and intelligent. She may rather snobbishly approve the young Greek professor's cultural prestige, but she knows that he is interested in the Salvation Army only because of Barbara. And she also cleverly divines his expensive tastes, thus preparing us for his subsequent daring demands. As regards Undershaft, again, she disapproves most heartily of some of his more radical sentiments, but she gives the devil his due with surprising accuracy.

Above all, she has no hesitation about speaking up for money. By contrast, Stephen, in Shaw's view, has more middle-class "romantic" views. Annoyed with his father, Stephen would refuse all subsidies. His mother would never be so foolhardy. Curiously enough, the Earl's daughter here reveals a realistic streak comparable to that of Undershaft, who will show an eminently hard-headed appreciation of the value of money. Stephen's view, on the other hand, will find its echo of sorts when the idealistic Barbara is later horrified to learn that the Salvation Army will accept contributions from manufacturers of guns and liquor.

## STEPHEN UNDERSHAFT

This very proper, fairly docile young product of England's famed Harrow and Cambridge serves two definite dramatic purposes in this first scene. For one thing he serves as comic foil for his mother. The more he nervously plays with tie and watch chain, the more she reproves him. And his game attempt to offer her "advice," as ordered, provokes an immediate, expected, but still amusing firm retort. In addition, he has been kept ignorant enough of the difficulties between his mother and his father so that he can ask a number of questions and thus enable Lady Britomart to furnish him and the audience with a wealth of expository material.

Stephen, however, has other aspects. He is, for instance, the young man of wealth, education and notable family background, who is all but devoid of special talent or creative ability. Whatever notions he has about life, he has accepted uncritically and holds to stubbornly. The prime example of Lady Britomart's tutelage, he has been "saved" from his father's independent thinking to become essentially a nonthinker. He is the nonproductive woman-dominated man, as contrasted with his father, who coolly refused to bow to his wife's ultimatum.

Among the philosophers whom Shaw read with interest was Auguste Comte, the 19th century French positivist. In picturing an ideal state Comte represents great industrialists as considering themselves trustees, running their plants for the good of others. These men do not leave their businesses to their sons, although providing well for their children. They choose instead the most capable individuals and train them as successors. (Kaye, *Shaw and the Nineteenth-Century Tradition*, pp. 44–45). In Shaw's play there is much made of the Undershaft tradition of adopting and training a "foundling" as heir. This is largely a fictional device, of dubious plausibility. Would the resolute, boldly independent Andrew Undershaft, herein described, be likely to follow slavishly a foolish old tradition? At the same time, it does point up Shaw's concern with the need for continuing progress. If the conventional system is followed, Lady Britomart's system, then Stephen, the incompetent, unquestioning, noncreative son, will succeed the dynamic man of vision. Progress will be halted, and gains will be sacrificed. So some way the deadlock must be broken, founding myth or no foundling myth, In this scene, Stephen, by toying with his watch chain, speaking up hesitantly, and generally yielding to his mother, would seem to be a convincing argument in favor of the Comtian idea of handing over key positions only to those with genuine potential for leadership.

Finally, Stephen is the "romantic" or the "idealist" type that Shaw often opposes. He imagines that a Greek scholar must of necessity have simple wants. As for himself, he has never wondered where the money came from for his support. Without knowing anything about his father's business, he has dismissed it as disagreeable. And upon learning that he has lived on munitions funds up to now, he rashly declares that he would die rather that ask for more money. Above all, he is astounded to be told that anyone cannot readily distinguish between right and wrong, thus failing to realize that some moral questions may be extremely complex. To Shaw a "romantic," in the undesirable sense, is one who has a false or unreal picture of life. In the course of the play Stephen, a very minor character, and his sister Barbara, a major one, will both lose certain illusions and learn to face certain facts more realistically. As of this first scene, however, Stephen, for all his education, is merely a pompous youth ill-prepared to solve any major problems, make any mark in the world, or even cope successfully with his assertive mother.

## PLOT DEVELOPMENT

In Shaw's plays the plot is seldom given primary emphasis, the interplay of ideas being much more important. Such plot as there is in this work concerns a conflict of views between *Major Barbara* Undershaft, of the Salvation Army, and her father, the munitions magnate. Her father will, in effect, try to prove to her that his way of life, regarded with such disapproval by his wife, Stephen, and many others, is really more contributory to human progress than her own as a Salvationist volunteer. There is little in the opening scene to prepare the audience for this duel. There is, however, the indication that the visit of Andrew to his family is an unprecedented one, and that he is a colorful and interesting personality. As for the matter of the girls' allowances, that is never going to be particularly important.

## SIGNIFICANT THEMES

### The Independent Genius

As described here, Andrew Undershaft, himself a foundling, has been bold and resourceful, has acquired great wealth and power, has married the daughter of the Earl of Stevenage and has successfully defeated her attempts to interfere with his plan to leave the business to someone qualified outside his own family. He has evidently supported his family with some generosity and has taken as his motto "Unashamed."

### The Possessive Woman

Lady Britomart, while not by any means impervious to Andrew's charm, essentially wanted a respectable and conventional husband who would automatically leave the business to their son. In Shaw's thinking the typical woman is primarily concerned with her children and with having a steady, unspectacular breadwinner to support them. Here Lady Britomart has secured the means for herself and her children but has obviously failed to stop her Shavian-hero husband from going on with his own activities in the way he sees fit.

### The Power of Great Wealth

Lady Britomart suggests that her husband's munitions industry controls Europe and is stronger than the law. Neither the government nor the press will try to interfere with him. Throughout the play Shaw will make much of the power of his arch-capitalist, especially as regards how this power can be harnessed to improve the lot of men in general.

### Flaws In Conventional Morality

In criticizing her husband, Lady Britomart says that she cannot tolerate an "immoral" man. To her, principles are all-important, regardless of how one behaves. Andrew practiced "morality," while preaching "immorality," and that she cannot forgive. For his part, Shaw seems much more impressed with solid achievements than with mere high-sounding hypocritical "principles."

### Limitations Of Conservatives

Stephen may glance at a Liberal weekly and Lady Britomart may deny proudly that hers is a "pig-headed Tory" family, but essentially both are not likely to favor much change or any new or progressive ideas. This is clear from Lady Britomart's critical comments about her unregimented husband and from Stephen's generally negative approach. Shaw, interested in Socialism and other movements, here treats satirically those who piously affirm that they "believe in liberty" but will normally do very little to improve the lot of others.

## ACT I, SCENE 2

### SUMMARY

> Having crushed Stephen's mild opposition, Lady Britomart sends Morrison, the butler, for the girls and their fiances. Entering with giddy, frivolous good humor, they are stunned to learn of Andrew's coming. Sarah acquiesces amiably, but Lomax makes fatuous comments to Lady Britomart's vast irritation. Cusins indulges in more subtly humorous

quips, and Barbara, in Salvation Army uniform, says that her father is welcome since he too has a soul to be saved. Lady Britomart warns all to be on their best behavior.

## Comment

This brief transitional scene serves three purposes. First of all, it introduces in person and differentiates the two Undershaft girls and their respective fiances. Secondly, by having Lady Britomart surprise them as she did Stephen with the announcement of her husband's visit, it builds up further a certain dramatic suspense regarding the arrival of the great man. Finally, like the opening scene, it offers light humor, with mild satiric overtones. The well-meant vapid remarks of the doltish Lomax vastly annoy the determined, virtually humorless Lady Britomart, who in turn is slyly ridiculed by the deceptively helpful Cusins.

## CHARACTER ANALYSIS

### Barbara Undershaft

In 1906, the Edwardian era, it would be customary for upper-class people to dress rather formally for dinner. Barbara, however, appears in her Salvation Army uniform. This departure from the usual would suggest three things about the girl, all of them valid in terms of the play's development.

First of all, she is a full-time salvationist. It would not be unusual in any period for a young lady of means to devote a few spare hours to charitable endeavors. But in wearing her uniform at a dinner party, Barbara indicates that her service with the Army is of paramount importance. Significantly enough, even when the young people were having a good time together before Lady Britomart's summons, Barbara, according to Cusins, was busy trying to teach him a Salvation Army march. And her first reaction to the news that her father is coming is that he, too, has a soul to save. Later, interestingly enough, when Barbara becomes disillusioned with the Army, the change will be startlingly represented by having her appear in ordinary fashionable attire.

Secondly, it sets her apart in a very special way from the others in the scene. Lady Britomart is anxious and slightly on edge about getting enough money so that her girls can live handsomely. She is being a good mother, in a sense, but her interests here are narrowly material. Sarah is casual, perhaps a bit bored. Lomax is a fool, and Cusins seems to be enjoying himself by quietly indulging his own taste for sardonic humor. But Barbara, in her uniform, hints of a world of serious concerns beyond that of the frivolous give-and-take in a comfortable town house. And her very reference to the problem of saving a soul makes her seem a young woman of enlightened interests. In general, Shaw has very little use for those who do not use their talents for the good of society. Great men and women, in his view, cooperate with the "Life-Force" by throwing themselves wholeheartedly into noble causes. As the play progresses, Shaw will point up certain deficiencies he believes to be in the program of the Salvation Army. And he will have his heroine alter her course. But from the first he shows her as at least trying to help humanity, even in some imperfect fashion, as opposed to those who never harbor any serious thoughts at all.

Lastly, she is being built up dramatically as a rather strong, independent personality, a worthy daughter of the resolute Andrew. Lady Britomart admits that Barbara likes to give orders and declares somewhat nervously that she will not be cowed or bullied by her daughter. Having made her entrance, Barbara calmly ignores the older woman's firm insistence that she stop calling Charles Lomax "Cholly." Nor is she at all fazed by the word of her father's coming, but sits on the edge of the table whistling "Onward Christian Soldiers." For all her bluster Lady Britomart always seems a trifle awed of her powerful husband. But Barbara, in identifying him promptly as a soul to be saved, seems wholly at ease. After all, in her view, she is an expert of sorts in soul-saving, and thus has a primary advantage. Before the play ends, Shaw will have her lose some of this cheerful assurance. But at this point she is being presented as a confident and worthy antagonist to debate the redoubtable Undershaft.

## LADY BRITOMART

In the previous scene Lady Britomart may have appeared at times comically wrong-headed, but she was triumphant. However absurd her claim to be only a woman needing advice, she did overwhelm the timorous Stephen. In this scene, however, the playwright pictures her as less forceful, still making pronouncements but being less heeded. For one thing, she admits being nervous about the upcoming interview and even loses the drift of her own statement at one point when attempting to rebuke Lomax. Barbara refuses her demand to stop calling Lomax "Cholly." Cusins, while pretending amiably to support her views, actually regards her with wry amusement. And her attempts to make much impression upon the obtuse Lomax are all but foredoomed, thus increasing her agitation.

Why has the playwright so modified the characterization? In the first place, her obviously rising uncertainty and anxiety provide further suspenseful preparation for the entrance of Undershaft. He will clearly be a much less easy conquest than

Stephen. Actually, Shaw is about to spring a clever surprise. For the rich and powerful Andrew will appear at first amazingly genial and meek. But in any play excitement over an approaching visit helps to rouse audience interest and expectations.

In addition, Lady Britomart must now in a sense abdicate in favor of Barbara. If there are to be vital confrontations in this play between a strong woman and a stronger man, the two involved are going to be Barbara and her father, not Lady Britomart and her husband. So now the peremptory and autocratic mother admits she can be cowed by a daughter who likes to give orders and may "bully" others. And Barbara, when told not to call Charles "Cholly," makes it quite clear that she has no intention of yielding readily to Lady Britomart. Shaw does not want two dominating female characters competing for attention. So Barbara here takes over the feminine lead.

If, however, Lady Britomart bows to Barbara, she also to some extent is downed by Adolphus Cusins, who, as Barbara's fiance, will figure prominently in the contest with Undershaft. In her efforts to prevent the inane Lomax from talking too much and thus making a bad impression upon Andrew, Lady Britomart is smoothly seconded by Cusins. But his straight-faced, gallant supporting speeches always suggest the tongue in cheek. Lady Britomart may miss the faint sarcasm, but the audience will take note of this cool, self-possessed young man, so different from the foolish Lomax.

## ADOLPHUS CUSINS

In his introductory notes Shaw describes Barbara's future husband as a slight young intellectual who wears glasses. Kindly and conscientious, he struggles against a hot temper and a tendency to be impatient and severely critical. Lady Britomart, in the previous scene, has already shrewdly suggested that Cusins attends Salvation Army meetings not because he is truly converted but because he wants to be near Barbara. Now when he talks of how funny it was when Barbara tried to teach him the "West Ham Salvation March," the same impression is created. Essentially, however, Cusins in this scene is revealed as a quiet-spoken, clever youth, remarkably articulate, with a subtle sense of humor. As was mentioned before, this character is said to have been based upon the Greek scholar, Gilbert Murray, whom Shaw much admired. And in the scene Cusins tosses in a brief **allusion** to Homer in the original, which much impresses his circle.

## CHARLES LOMAX

Represented as a frivolous young man about town, Cholly, in an effort to be agreeable, usually says the wrong thing. He also uses slang in a manner that appalls Lady Britomart and is not above a few slips in grammar. Dramatically he too serves several purposes. First of all, he is a comic character. British drawing-room comedies or comedies of manners often boasted a silly, foppish youth at whom the audience could laugh, even if condescendingly. Secondly, he sets off by contrast the educated, wittier Adolphus. Finally, in terms of Shaw's social thinking, he is one more argument against the usual system of passing down usable wealth to one's heirs regardless of capabilities. Cholly will have 800 pounds a year until he is 35 and will then inherit a million. But Lady Britomart, who has selected him as an appropriate husband for Sarah, has no illusions as to his general competence. In fact, she has said that if he did try to make money, he would probably lose what he had already. In addition, she harshly ridicules his lame and rather silly efforts to comment on the impending visit. As a product of any system, then, Lomax is certainly no argument against some sort of radical change. As a social thinker, Shaw can suggest no good reason for entrusting vast wealth to inept drones such as this.

## SIGNIFICANT THEME

### Salvation

Barbara says that her father will be welcome as a visitor because he has a soul to save. This whole question of "salvation" will be a vital question in later scenes. At one crucial point, for example, Undershaft will claim to have saved Barbara, and she in turn will have tried to convert the truculent Bill Walker. Shaw's concept of salvation may not necessarily coincide with that of orthodox religions, but this will still be a principal theme.

## TOPIC FOR DISCUSSION

Is Shaw's handling of the young people convincing? In general, he seems to disapprove of devoting one's self to lighthearted convivial pleasures. More than one critic has noted his Puritanical impatience with time-killing pleasures and his inability to understand their appeal. So does he tend to make his high-spirited quartet almost childishly silly? Or would adequate staging make the scene seem genuinely comic?

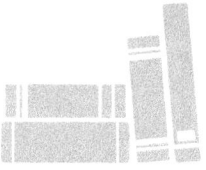

# MAJOR BARBARA

## TEXTUAL ANALYSIS

## ACT 1, SCENES 3 AND 4; ACT 2, SCENE 1

### ACT I, SCENE 3

#### SUMMARY

Ushered in by a nonplussed Morrison, the genial and deceptively meek Undershaft seems at first comically unsure which of the young people are his children. Once properly introduced by Cusins, he argues with Lomax and Stephen about the merits of munitions-making and takes a lively interest in Barbara and her work. He accepts her invitation to visit her shelter with the understanding that she in turn will visit his factory. Lomax plays his concertina, but Lady Britomart breaks up the pleasant gathering by insisting upon family prayers.

| Comment

After some rather awkward farcical confusion of identities, Barbara and her father are finally brought face to face to deliver their respective challenges. The scene essentially is Undershaft's, revealing not only his forceful personality but his characteristic attitudes toward armaments and war, religion and music.

## CHARACTER ANALYSIS

### Andrew Undershaft

Apparently uncertain at first as to which of the five young people are his progeny, Undershaft still appears gracious, charming, and assured. He is clearly a man used to handling difficult situations. At the same time, he is quick to appreciate the helpful clarification provided by Cusins. All the while he treats his wife, Lady Britomart, with Old World courtliness, despite her efforts to be cordially businesslike. He mentions once, almost proudly, that he is an uneducated man. But as he greets each in turn, he reveals impeccable poise.

When a conversational lull prompts Barbara to call upon Lomax for a concertina solo, Undershaft reveals that he, too, is much interested in music. As a poor boy he danced for money and later played the tenor trombone. The references here to music have several curious aspects. For one thing, Shaw himself was passionately fond of various types. His mother was a teacher of singing, and he himself studied voice and piano. In addition he had served for two years as music critic on *The Star* (1888–1890) and four years on *The World* (1890–1894). Moreover, as a playwright, he first became intrigued with the idea of a work about the Salvation Army after publicly defending the Army's bands against certain slurs by a newspaper writer.

Since, then, Undershaft is in many ways an admirable figure to Shaw, it is not surprising that he shares the musical interests of the playwright. Moreover, the discussion leads to a musical interlude in this scene and looks ahead to an effective use of marching hymns in the shelter scene. Finally, in having his munitions king talk of step dancing and trombone playing, Shaw not only points up the fact of his being a determined self-made man but also works to shake the confidence of such conventionally prejudiced people as Lomax that they know all there is to know about the powerful men who mold their destinies.

If, however, Undershaft indicates a musical bent, he also startles the family group by claiming a profound interest in religion. Intelligent enough to recognize an opportunity, even if there is a curious challenge here, the ardent Barbara invites him to her shelter. Lomax, however, is thoroughly confused. Cholly, who considers it "bad form" to belong to anything but the Established Church, cannot see how a cannon maker can be religious at all, since cannon-making, while necessary, is morally wrong. His only suggested loophole is that perhaps Undershaft, by making weapons more and more destructive, will eventually make war undesirable. But the industrialist will have none of such wishful thinking. He expects wars to continue and has no pious wish at all to go bankrupt through universal peace. If therefore he is a "religious" and a "moral" man, as he maintains he is, his religion and morality must be quite different from the Christianity at least nominally subscribed to by Lomax and Stephen. His further statement that everyone must follow his own individual "true morality" outrages his already hostile son. He does not elaborate further at this point, but Barbara, preferring to overlook the complexities of his view, says merely that all sinners need the same salvation and repeats her invitation.

In the course of the brief discussion of religion, several other characteristics of Undershaft become apparent. Remaining courteous and unruffled throughout, he is always the master of the situation. He is also intellectually agile, although, in fairness, it must be admitted the young people are not unusually astute. More than this, he has apparently done considerable thinking about fundamentals and worked out his own unorthodox but personally satisfying system. He is attractive enough. Even apart from her missionary aspirations, his vital and charming daughter obviously likes him. As they exit together, her arm is about him. Yet, although only hints are offered here, there is, too, a cool, deliberate ruthless element in this genial, elderly tycoon. From the first, regardless of Barbara's sanguine hopes, he is a strong man more likely to convert than to be converted.

Two notes may be added as to the character's source. Shaw once told his biographer, Henderson, that he got the idea for the character from a gentle and benevolent older neighbor, who, Shaw was startled to discover, manufactured explosives. The possibilities of dramatic contrast fascinated the future creator of Undershaft. In addition, Shaw's audiences might well have heard of the actual church of St. Andrew Undershaft in London. The "undershaft" in the title came from the early practice of putting up the shaft of the spring maypole annually in front of the building. Furthermore, Shaw admired many of the writings on social theories by Thomas Carlyle. Carlyle has a mythical capitalist, whom he calls Plugson of Undershot, because he comes from the mythical parish of St. Dolly Undershot. Barbara, of course, often shortens Cusins' name Adolphus to "Dolly." So there may be some intended echo. (See Kaye, *Bernard Shaw and the Nineteenth-Century Tradition*, note on p. 15.)

## BARBARA UNDERSHAFT

Three characteristics of Barbara are brought out in this scene. She is, first of all, heartier and freer in her manner than Sarah, the more usual Edwardian young lady. In the previous scene she sat on the table and quietly whistled. Now, to her mother's horror, she tells Cholly Lomax that releasing his suppressed laughter would be good for his "inside." Secondly, she is imperious or managerial. At the end, despite Lady Britomart's call for family prayers, she sweeps off her father and summons Cusins and Lomax. Finally, she is again the ardent Salvation Army leader. She tells of trying to interest Lomax and confidently invites Undershaft to the shelter. She also gladly accepts his bid to see his foundry, having no doubt that her religion will impress the maker of cannons. Here she is young, optimistic, and somewhat naive. She may have, as she rather grandly states, had scores of "scoundrels, criminals," and "infidels" confess their sinfulness at her shelter. But Undershaft, who is positive, wily, and a missionary of sorts for his own radical notions, will prove a far more formidable challenger.

## CHARLES LOMAX

The character of Lomax here is developed somewhat differently in comparison with the previous scene. Although no marvel as an original thinker, Lomax is far more articulate as he argues with Undershaft than would have been suspected as he uttered nervous, embarrassed ejaculations before to the vast irritation of Lady Britomart. He is given fairly conventional views to state so that they may be provocatively answered by Undershaft. But in this exchange Lomax is far less of the silly oaf. Why is the change made? Obviously when Lomax acts idiotically-and he will again, later on-the actor captures the audience's attention and gets laughs. Here, however, Shaw wants heed paid to the ideas voiced by Undershaft. So Cholly must merely set up the problem and then cease to offer humorous distraction. Incidentally, he also is made useful by being unexpectedly credited with proficiency on the concertina.

## SIGNIFICANT THEMES

### Realism Vs. Romanticism

Lomax, having affirmed his belief that making cannons is immoral, is suddenly face to face with a future father-in-law who makes guns. To gloss over the situation, he hopefully suggests that perhaps the arms manufacturer is really developing terrible weapons to abolish war the more rapidly. This to Undershaft and/or Shaw is a "romantic" notion. Undershaft as a "realist" says first that people will be even more fascinated with deadlier weapons and second that he has no wish to see a peace that would put an end to all his profits. He will thus be satisfied with no hypocritical evasion.

### Flaws In Conventional Religion

In speaking up for his trade, Undershaft declares that he puts his profits into further research for improving his guns, not into hospitals, churches, and other "receptacles for conscience money." Moreover, he will have none of Christianity's counsel to accept injuries meekly, since then no one would buy weapons. He has his own version of the Salvation Army's motto of "Blood and Fire." There is little development of the Undershaft idea here. But in the next Act both criticisms will be developed further. Much money spent for charitable "good works" only helps to perpetuate conditions of social injustice. And, secondly, encouraging humble acceptance of evils holds up movements that might change the whole picture by energetic effort.

## TOPICS FOR DISCUSSION

1. Would any people today, do you think, share the feeling of Lomax that the business of manufacturing dangerous weapons is both necessary and immoral?

2. Is Undershaft right in labeling by inference industrial contributions to hospitals and other charitable institutions "conscience money"? Has the situation changed from that of Shaw's early twentieth century?

3. Is Shaw justified in altering somewhat the personality of a minor character like Lomax from scene to scene to suit other purposes? How desirable is consistency in such portrayals?

## ACT I, SCENE 4

### SUMMARY

Barbara leaves with her father, followed by Lomax. Lady Britomart tries to hold Adolphus but is adroitly dissuaded. Then having dismissed him and the bored Sarah, she bursts into tears before Stephen. He tries to console her that she has not lost her children's affection, but she flounces out to join the rest. He remains alone in angry protest, as strains of a hymn on concertina with tambourine are heard from the drawing room.

## Comment

In their initial appearances, Lady Britomart comes in like a lion, Undershaft like a lamb. And Barbara always seems good-natured, quietly assured. This scene leaves no doubt as to where the balance of power lies. Lady Britomart may say that she will not be disobeyed. But one by one all but Stephen follow Barbara and her father to the drawing-room, even the great lady herself. This would seem to be a clear indication that whatever of moment happens from now on in the play, Barbara's mother is not likely to be a prime mover.

## CHARACTER ANALYSIS

### Lady Britomart

The teary outburst of the autocratic matriarch is understandable enough. She has tried to compel the family and guests to attend family prayers and been neatly and successfully checkmated. There is fear, however, as well as frustration. Lady Britomart, always primarily the mother, broke initially with her husband because she thought he was denying rights to their son. She has now, after all these years, asked him to call in order to insure a more comfortable life for her two engaged daughters. And now the girls, at least, seem to be deserting her for Andrew.

Interestingly enough, as the critic Arthur Nethercot has pointed out, her idea of motherhood is almost totally negative. A mother is one who denies, restrains and punishes (Nethercot, *Men and Supermen*, p. 101). Yet apparently she craves "affection." At the same time, she has no patience with herself for showing any feminine weakness and brushes off angrily even the loyal Stephen's well-meant attempts to reassure her. She may sometimes actually feel like "only a woman," but she long ago became wary of masculine charm. Undershaft she used to find "clever and unanswerable" even when he argued in favor of whatever she considered wicked. He was "very attractive" and she "did not dislike him." In fact, he seems sometimes to have almost won her over for the moment with his "affectionate nonsense." So Lady Britomart has been on her guard since he arrived, rejecting as "Rubbish!" his courtly opening compliment. The idea, however, of using charm herself as a countermeasure seems never to occur to her. She relies ever upon strength, resolution, and a conviction of being solidly in the right.

Still in her own way she is a "realist." Once, however frustratingly, she realizes the true situation, she is not one to waste time in fruitless tears. If the group is in the drawing room, she will go there, too.

### Adolphus Cusins

Again the young scholar's breezy self-confidence is apparent as he glibly explains why he cannot stay for family prayers. His argument runs that all would have to admit having done things that were wrong, and that this would be unfair to Lady Britomart, to Barbara, and to himself. The older woman, of course, is neither convinced nor particularly mollified by his ingenious explanation. She takes the occasion, in fact, to warn him that she knows, if Barbara does not, that his attendance at Salvation Army meetings is strictly to worship Barbara. In any event, the incident proves once more that Cusins has a mind of his own. He will not even sit down when Lady Britomart so commands, even though he is never obviously rude. Secondly, both in avoiding the family prayers and in not denying wherein lies his true concern with the Salvation Army, he indicates a skeptical attitude toward religion, at least in its more conventional forms. Finally, he is reasonably cool and resourceful. He can find an argument or a quotation for any course he wants to defend, and he is no daunted by Lady Britomart's assertion that she sees through his pretended enthusiasm for the Salvation Army. By the end of the play, Cusins, the slight, bespectacled professor of Greek, will be designated the heir and successor of the dynamic Andrew Undershaft. In these early scenes certain traits are revealed that will make this apparently unlikely choice seem more plausible.

## Stephen Undershaft

At this stage, Stephen remains totally unimpressed with the charm and magnetism of his father. Of course, he tends in general to side with his mother, who has only recently informed him of Undershaft'seplan to deprive him of his customary "rights" as son and heir. Apart from this, however, he resents his father's contention that there may be more than one true morality and true religion. Stephen has a doggedly conservative mind that rejects angrily any suggestion that there may be alternative points of view. He has almost no intellectual curiosity and even less flexibility. When even his mother follows Undershaft and Barbara into the drawing room, he stubbornly and bitterly remains alone. Again it must be emphasized that the conversion of Stephen Undershaft, while it will eventually be achieved, is not a vital matter in the play. Stephen will never in any real sense carry on any Undershaft tradition. As a minor character, however, he is useful to Shaw, as was Lomax in the previous scene, as a striking example of what is wrong with England's upper classes. Shaw is all in favor of receptivity to new ideas, independence of spirit, and the energetic and daring pursuit of challenging enterprises. He favors progress in all areas, and this demands a willingness to re-examine and possibly change conventional convictions. But while Undershaft and Barbara will at least investigate each other's claims, Stephen sullenly resists every attempt to stimulate questioning. He is the champion of the status quo.

## SIGNIFICANT THEMES

### Puritanism

Lady Britomart paints a rather dismal picture of parenthood with her emphasis upon restraining children, giving them tasks and punishing them. She has also rebuked Barbara for suggesting that religion could be something "pleasant." Shaw, himself, of course, has been called puritanical. But it must not be assumed that he necessarily sides with the often wrongheaded Lady Britomart in suggesting that what is worthwhile must be disagreeable. Shaw is a Puritan in the sense that he believes that there is much to be done to promote human progress and that to spend one's life in frivolous pleasure-seeking is a dreadful waste. But if religion has value or other pursuits are useful, the music-minded playwright will certainly not object to their being accompanied by song. He himself as a platform speaker on behalf of Fabian socialism was noted for his wit and unfailing good temper.

### Flaws In Conventional Religion

In turning down Lady Britomart's summons to family prayers, Cusins takes issue with those affirmations of sinfulness that are conducive to humility. To some extent, of course, this is a joke. It is an ingenious excuse for joining the other young people offered by a mentally dexterous opportunist. Yet there are two interesting aspects to the passage. First of all, there is the question of hypocrisy. Undershaft's motto is "unashamed," and he will have nothing to do with "conscience money." Cusins, too, says that he is doing his best, and that is that. Actually, however, although Lady Britomart once denied being a Pharisee and admitted that no one is perfect, she does not really act as though she thought she were in any way morally guilty. On the contrary, everything she says suggests that she holds a pretty high opinion of her own rectitude. So for her to go on reciting the formulas for prayers of humility is an essential contradiction, there being no indication that she truly means what she says. Hence, the passage represents one more brief attempt by Shaw to suggest that those who call themselves religious do not always practice what they preach.

In addition, Shaw is always ready to attack any element in Christianity, as he knows it, that emphasizes submissiveness or humility. Again it will be noted that the Undershaft key word is "Unashamed." Shaw refers to all in traditional religion that advocates meekness as "Crosstianity," a term of contempt. His idea is that such an attitude helps to unjust to remain well-entrenched and encourages the oppressed to remain passive victims. Hence, it is not surprising that in selecting some prayers for Cusin's humorous rejection, Shaw would pick those in which the Christian calls himself unworthy.

## ACT II, SCENE 1

### SUMMARY

The next morning, outside the Army's bleak slum shelter in West Ham, a thinly clad pair consume a skimpy meal of bread, syrup, and skim milk. Snobby Price, an able-bodied painter, more given to talk than work, sneers at capitalist charity. Rummy Mitchens, another Cockney, in her forties, speaks kindly, if condescendingly of the volunteers. Both admit they have shamelessly invented lurid pasts and lied about conversions to go on being fed at the shelter.

## Comment

In presenting this somewhat cynical exchange between Snobby and Rummy as the scene changes to the shelter, Shaw does little to create a favorable impression of the Army's spiritual effectiveness. It is an amusing enough scene. The Cockney dialect is used for its comic values, and there is, of course, something droll about these two skilled "promoters" so expert about supplying dramatic if fraudulent confessions for some free food. In addition, Shaw is developing certain ideas through this picturesque pair as to what is wrong with the approach to the problem of poverty in the England of his time.

## CHARACTER ANALYSIS

### Snobby Price

Although boasting grandly of his prowess as a "real painter: grainer, finisher," Snobby obviously prefers a life of relative leisure. Believing himself brainier than his fellow-craftsmen, he adds loftily that his father, a stationer, was a Chartist. During the early 19th century English workers took part in the Chartist movement to secure universal manhood suffrage and other political rights. The movement failed, but its objectives were eventually realized. Shaw, in general, would not find the Chartist program ideal. For one thing, of course, it had proved ineffectual.

But essentially Shaw did not want to extend the vote and leave the over-all system unchanged. He wanted to substitute a form of socialism for capitalism. In any event, he would not favor adoption of social theories mainly to give oneself airs. Snobby merely uses his father's interest in Chartism as one more lame excuse for not sullying his hands with work. And Shaw always insists that the worthwhile individual in any class must make good use of his opportunities for service.

Snobby argues further that in a country in which the leaders were sober, hard-working, and honest, he would follow suit. As it is, he is merely following the prevailing custom by drinking, idling and stealing whatever he can without getting caught. As in Cusins' criticism of family prayers. Shaw has more than one purpose here. Snobby is, to some extent, a comic character, and his clever rationalization is funny. Whatever others do, he is merely thinking up ingenious excuses for not overstraining himself. He even adds, with spurious concern for his fellows, that he does not want to deprive someone else of a job by taking it himself. At the same time, Shaw probably would accept some of Snobby's strictures on English upper class life. In his works he is clearly not satisfied with the efforts of such as Lady Britomart, Sarah and Lomax to further human progress.

## Rummy Mitchens

Although seemingly more frail and destitute than Snobby, Rummy is almost as much of a fraud. She loftily insists upon due respect as a respectable married woman, yet she is prepared to dream up a melodramatic account of sin and shame to please the good-hearted volunteers and keep the shelter going. Her only regret is that out of mistaken consideration for frailer vessels, the Salvation Army lasses frown upon sensational public confessions by women. This restriction distresses Rummy, for she thinks apparently that it would be rather exciting to be the center of attraction having concocted a fantastic life history. Incidentally, she admits that her mother named her Romola. Shaw's audiences would probably recognize the name as that of the noble Florentine heroine in George Eliot's novel of that name. The contrast is amusing, as it is when Snobby admits that he too has a highly romantic first name, Bronterre.

## SIGNIFICANT THEMES

### Romanticism Vs. Realism

Shaw here works to shatter the illusions of all who regard the poor as universally humble, pious, and pathetically grateful for whatever charity bestows. These two are shrewdly taking advantage of their credulous benefactors, Snobby with ill-concealed contempt, Rummy with condescending sympathy.

### Evils Of Poverty

Shaw is said to have first developed his hatred of slum miseries when as a child he was taken by nursemaids on visits to their friends in Dublin's poorer sections. In any case, he does not suggest that the situation of Rummy and Snobby is a desirable one. The January morning is bitterly cold, and they are inadequately clothed. Their scant breakfast consists of a slice of bread with syrup and a mug of thin milk.

To get this they are demeaning themselves with lying confessions. In Shaw's ideal society both would be well fed, well clothed and well housed. And Snobby would be working as a painter, not talking about it. They would then have more dignity and independence. Under the present system, they do not starve, but neither do they do much to achieve a satisfactory life for themselves or others.

## Flaws In Conventional Religion

The Salvation Army, in Shaw's view, has excellent intentions and, what's more, makes an honest effort to help people. Barbara, obviously, is more admirable as a person than the languid, insipid Sarah. But the Army, through its insistence upon "conversions," supported by emotional "confessions," encourages, says Shaw, this kind of callous deception. In addition, the meager rations merely help prolong misery and do little to remove the causes. By encouraging the poor to accept their lot, the Army, he feels, allies itself with the "Crosstianity," that Shaw so loathes.

## TOPIC FOR DISCUSSION

Some claim that Shaw tips the scales unfairly by introducing two such unscrupulous fakers as Rummy and Snobby. Do you agree? Or is he justified in selecting whatever evidence supports his point of view?

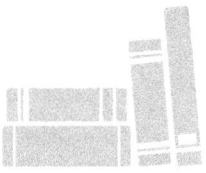

# MAJOR BARBARA

## TEXTUAL ANALYSIS

## ACT 2, SCENES 2–4

### ACT II, SCENE 2

#### SUMMARY

Jenny Hill, a pale, tired, very young volunteer, brings out Peter Shirley, a starving, unemployed workman. She gives him food, as Rummy and Snobby offer hypocritically pious greetings. Then Bill Walker, a rough, aggressive young Cockney, arrives to demand furiously of Jenny that she send out for a beating his former love, Mog Habbijam, who left him when the Army converted her. Failing to get his way, he strikes Rummy, threatens Snobby, and after dragging Jenny by the hair, gives her face a smashing blow.

#### Comment

Although Shaw's plays are often said to consist largely of good talk or spirited debates, there sometimes occurs a scene such as this in which there is physical action or even violence. Bill Walker is not one to argue a point quietly. Stung because he lost his girl to the Salvationist group, he is prepared to reassert his rights with his fist. The scene is a lively one, and most audiences tend to feel sorry for the innocent victim, pretty young Jenny Hill. Shaw, however, is busy setting up a situation that will enable him to convey certain theories of his one crime and punishment. By the time he finishes with the young culprit we will have perhaps more pity for the simple ruffian than we first had for the poor girl he brutally slams.

## CHARACTER ANALYSIS

Peter Shirley: A genuine hardship case, Peter represents the "deserving" as opposed to the "undeserving" poor. Unlike the glibly rationalizing Snobby, Peter really wants to work. Although he looks older, he claims to be only in his mid-forties and talks harshly of a system that will deny employment, merely because of a gray streak in his hair, to a man who has labored hard all his life. Again, unlike the other two, he is distressed at the idea of accepting charity. Even though he is ravenous, he will eat only when assured that he can pay back the Army once it has found him a job. In this case, the Army would seem to be providing valuable help. The man is starving. Yet again, Shaw is eyeing critically a system that will place a workman in so humiliating a position.

Snobby Price: Snobby's unctuous words of cheer to the new arrival, Peter, point up his own comical hypocrisy and, more seriously, the weaknesses in the Army structure that encourage this type of shameless prevaricating, In addition, Snobby here is shown up as a coward. Not totally devoid of chivalry, despite his rancor toward capitalists, he protests mildly when Bill Walker shoves Jenny. But when Walker starts threatening him, he immediately retreats. Incidentally, in the previous scene the humorous point was made that actually instead of beating his old mother, as the dramatically avows in his trumped-up confession he was usually beaten by his old mother. Apart from the amusement derived by the reader from watching the braggart hastily slink off, the incident illustrates even more vividly how little the Army's teaching really means to such an opportunist. He may assure Shirley that at the shelter will be found rest and peace and understanding and Jenny that here he has obtained a peace beyond all expectations. But let personal danger impend, he will quickly abjure all interest in the kindly volunteer.

Bill Walker: At this stage Bill is mainly the bully. Stronger physically than any of the others, he is ready to rain blows on all who thwart his purposes. He does not make any distinctions on the basis of age, sex, or frailty. He will strike old Rummy or tired, young Jenny without compunction. And his object is coming is to administer a salutary drubbing to the girl who left him when she found salvation. Incidentally, he does not seem passionately attached to the defecting Mog, nor does he indicate that he wants her back. He merely wants to avenge his own hurt pride. In a curious way, it is to him a matter of principle, and within a short time he will have much more complex matters of principle to consider. At this point Bill could literally not live with himself if he allowed such an affront to pass without proper retribution. Later when he has been made to feel guilt for the blow to Jenny, he will again have to find some way of meeting his own personal standards before he can achieve again a sense of well-being. Snobby Price is a less abusive but more shallow offender. There is no suggestion that he is ever going to commit any big offense or suffer any particular remorse. But Bill Walker, the ruffian who strikes defenseless women, is a character with greater spiritual potential. In a very interesting study comparing *Major Barbara* and Dante's *Divine Comedy*, a critic, Joseph Frank, suggests that Bill's problem of personal expiation must be carefully considered for any true understanding of Shaw's basic thinking.

Jenny Hill: Jenny, the pale young Salvation Army lass, is shown here to be hard-working, ardent, sincere, kindly, and naive. She obviously has no suspicions when Snobby and Rummy echo hollowly her own exalted religious sentiments. She is extremely conscientious, feeling guilty for not doing more, even though she is already close to exhaustion. But she is humanly very frightened when Bill Walker talks to her so menacingly and later strikes her brutally. In comparison with Barbara Undershaft, Jenny is a rather simple young girl. Both are putting forth their best efforts to do good, as they see it. But the daughter of Undershaft and the granddaughter of the Earl of Stevenage is a much more forceful and perceptive individual. Barbara does not frighten easily. She can, in fact, be quite formidable. Yet being deeper, she will never, like Jenny, be able to go on with her Army work once she has been educated as to some of its contradictions.

## SIGNIFICANT THEMES

### Evils Of Poverty

Peter Shirley, who is already cold and weak from hunger, must further endure the humiliation of accepting charity. His self-respect is threatened by his being forced in effect to beg in order to survive. Jenny Hill is kind and sympathetic, but the experience is still a painful one for Peter.

### Evils Of Capitalism

From the age of thirteen on, according to Shirley, he has worked long hours only to be summarily discharged once his hair shows signs of graying. To Shaw there is something wrong with a "laissez faire" or unregulated industrial system that can be callously wasteful of human potential. Shirley is apparently not lazy. He is willing to contribute. Presumably under a better system he would go on being gainfully employed and thus be spared the misery he now painfully endures.

### Flaws In Conventional Religion

According to Shaw, it encourages hypocrisy, as in the insincere protestations of Rummy and Snobby. It does save the life of a man like Shirley, but it also keeps in operation the system that forced him out of work without any way of supporting himself.

### TOPIC FOR DISCUSSION

Does the fact that the audience has been permitted to learn the real sentiments of Snobby and Rummy make this scene more amusing and more effective? Would there have been any dramatic advantage in introducing Peter Shirley before the two pious frauds?

## ACT II, SCENE 3

### SUMMARY

> As Jenny leaves, sobbing with pain, Shirley angrily confronts Walker, brandishing his mug. Disliking all young men as job rivals, Shirley denounces him for striking down only the weak. He dares him to take on a young relative, Todger Fair-mile, the noted wrestler. Bill dislikes the prospect and decides to go in after his girl. Shirley warns him that he will have to reckon with an Earl's granddaughter.

## Comment

Just as Snobby retreated when menaced by the truculent Bill, so that worthy is shown to be not altogether without fear. Dramatically, of course, it is an interesting surprise to have the weak and tottering Shirley stand up so boldly to the allconquering Walker. And it is also startling and, naturally, amusing when the powerful savage seems somewhat cowed. Afterwards Shirley follows up his advantage by frightening his adversary with alarming reference to an invincible relative and to a lady of great influence who can probably have him arrested for assault. The scene, however, also has its element of pathos. When Walker taunts Shirley about accepting charity, the latter tearfully admits that he is only a poor man rejected by society. One other point may be mentioned. Observing that Bill has been drinking gin, Shirley predicts that Walker himself will soon be ruined and forced also to beg for his bread. Walker, however, denies that he drinks steadily. He merely did so this time to nerve himself up to beat Mog. Much will subsequently be made of Walker's conscience. This small admission of his somehow prepares for later developments by making him appear less instinctively brutal. The references to gin-drinking as hastening the impoverishment of such men as Walker also look ahead to the next scenes in which the name of Bodger, the whiskey distiller, will figure prominently. Shaw himself, like Shirley, was a teetotaler.

## CHARACTER ANALYSIS

### Peter Shirley

Once revived with food, Shirley shows considerable spirit in facing up to the menacing Bill. Probably this is partly due to a certain native shrewdness. Shirley has spotted the fact that Bill has been drinking and suspects-accurately, as it turns out-that his bellowing truculence may by now be petering out. As a teetotaler, Shirley seems to feel a certain superiority to gin drinkers anyway. In addition, Shirley has accurately sized up the true situation at the shelter and knows that Bill, for all his bombast is probably no match for the formidable granddaughter of an Earl. But most of all, Shirley is aggrievedly conscious of the fact that he has lost his job to younger men. Hence, The has a special animus against young Bill the minute the latter starts making trouble. The aggressive Walker, in other words, suddenly rouses all of Shirley's pent-up bitterness against a whole class of young people who have reduced him to penury. And this animosity is violent enough to nerve him to defy the insolent bully. On Shaw's part this is an interesting bit of psychological analysis. It also points up anew the injustices of a system that is, in human terms, cruel and wasteful.

## Bill Walker

The invincible scourge of West Ham, although still sputtering, retreats visibly as Shirley opposes him with his own incongruously ferocious stance, with the ominous prowess of Todger Fairmile, and with the possible political influence of *Major Barbara*. Always anxious to stand up for his rights, not to mention his own manhood, Bill is still Cockney realist enough to know that he is no match for the professionals. Intriguingly enough, he is also curiously sensitive. Shirley's taunts about striking only the defenseless do make him uneasy. In a scene that follows, Barbara will expertly rouse his conscience. It becomes subtly evident here, however, that he really has a conscience to rouse.

## SIGNIFICANT THEMES

### Evils Of Capitalism

Again Shirley drives home the idea that he has been cruelly and senselessly discarded in favor of younger workers. In this way Shaw shows the system then operating in England as incapable of providing adequately for the aging worker. Shirley presumably is still capable of earning his keep. Why then should a self-respecting man have to beg for bread and treacle? asks the playwright.

### Evils Of Drinking

Shirley argues that young men like Walker, who drink, will be deprived of livelihoods and reduced to beggary even before they are as old as he is. Bill denies, in effect, that he is a habitual alcoholic. But as subsequent scenes will indicate, Shaw, who does not drink, links the liquor and armaments industries as equally destructive.

## ACT II, SCENE 4

### SUMMARY

A casual, pleasant, and matter-of-fact Barbara enters and seeks information from Shirley, promising to find him a job. As to religion, he firmly claims to be a Secularist. Turning to Bill, she adroitly deflates him. The bruised Jenny Hill, she says, prays for him, and his conscience is sure to give him trouble. She then tells him that the converted Mog has a new

> love, Todger Fairmile, the wrestler. This completes Bill's discomfiture.

## Comment

The scene gives us *Major Barbara* in action. With superb aplomb and more than a touch of aristocratic condescension, she wins over Shirley and thoroughly unsettles the insolent Walker, already shaken by the old pauper's dire warnings. This is Barbara at her best as Lady Bountiful. Cheerful and confident, she is completely in command of the situation. As a dramatist, Shaw is setting her up for a later disillusioning experience that will shatter all this sunny assurance, only to restore it later as she moves on to what the playwright considers a more promising field of endeavor. At this point, however, she is as positive as Lady Britomart.

## CHARACTER ANALYSIS

### Barbara Undershaft

As she briskly writes down Shirley's data in her notebook, Barbara is efficient, kindly, and sensible. Not at all surprised that Shirley has lost his job, she takes up the matter of his dyeing his hair. Then, having ascertained that he is a "steady," nondrinking worker, she seems certain that she can help him find work. She is not only perceptive but tactful. Upon inquiring about Shirley's religion, she encounters unexpected hostility. Shirley claims to be a Secularist, that is, one who rejects religious faith and worship. Realizing quickly that she has encountered resistance, she immediately assures him that her own father probably shares his general persuasion. This is probably an instinctive association, but it is also one that is highly flattering to the poor workman she is trying to convert. The audience knows from previous scenes that Shirley is very much impressed with Barbara's status as a member of the aristocracy. He has quite astutely used her name and position as threats to cow Walker. So her talking of him and of her father in the same breath is a very effective way of dissolving his antagonism.

At the same time she quietly suggests that God in some way is using this secularist belief of his for some good purpose. This type of almost maddening certainty leaves Shirley somewhat baffled. But, having made her first tentative move to win him over, she lets him alone and turns to the recalcitrant Walker.

In handling Bill, her airy, offhand manner again proves unsettling. Those familiar with other Shaw plays may with interest compare Barbara's tactics in this scene with those of the cool and exasperating Ann Whiteside in *Man and Superman*. For regardless of the religious and other matters here under discussion, Barbara is a young, lovely, and tantalizing woman reducing a bewildered young man to exasperation, while apparently being nothing but sweet, sympathetic, and reasonable. If she called Bill names or even lost her temper he would happily know how to retort with gusto. He has no trouble later on exchanging insults with Rummy Mitchens. But a serene, friendly, authoritative personality who infallibly analyzes his problems and even presumes to predict his very conscience twinges is enough to distract any poor, ordinary brute.

In this scene, Barbara, like Lady Britomart, seems to be completely sure of herself and of her beliefs. She is also, of course, the ardent missionary, eager to save every soul she encounters. Her attitude toward the two men is thus one of the blissfully saved to the still lost sheep. Actually, she tries to bridge the gap by assuming a comradely air of hearty fellowship. She puts Peter and her father in the same class, just as she had previously assured Undershaft that she was familiar with all types of sinners, finding them remarkably similar. With the same jaunty manner, she will talk to Walker about Mog's having found herself a new "bloke." But the class barrier is always there, and the air of condescension unmistakable. The play, of course, was written over a half-century ago, when English society was far more rigidly stratified. A lady was a lady, and a bloke a bloke. But in terms of the play, it must never be forgotten that the admirable but rather brash Barbara has boldly challenged her father, the wily and determined Undershaft. And Shaw is now letting her put to rout minor adversaries only to be routed in turn by a more powerful one. He has, incidentally, used this technique twice before. He let Lady Britomart overwhelm Stephen only to yield to Barbara and Cusins. He also let Bill triumph momentarily and then let both Shirley and Barbara break down his truculent air of bravado.

### Bill Walker

Already somewhat shaken by the triple onslaught of Shirley in the previous scene, Bill emerges here as the virtually hopeless but still stubborn defender of a lost cause. Deserted by his girl, he has gone on the rampage and been branded a cowardly assaulter of the weak. Barbara can have him arrested, and Todger Fairmile can beat him up. What is more, the insistent Barbara contends that Mog, her red hair now newly washed, is happy after her conversion since she has the love of Todger. And furthermore, she predicts nothing but qualms of conscience for the already miserable Bill. When he dragged and struck Jenny, Bill was an unlovely character. But now as he dolefully tries a few blustery threats and insults, he acquires a curious air of gallantry. In some ways, of course, Bill is almost a child, an angry, sullen, violent unruly individual. And this may justify Barbara's patient maternal, even soothing approach. But there is something at once pathetic and comic about this beleaguered ruffian as he gamely tries to answer the unanswerable. Barbara, of course, has shrewdly discovered his vulnerability and mercilessly pursued her advantage. Bill can only stand dolefully alone, defying almost in despair a combination of cruel fates. He is a sad figure, because he is, in a sense, trapped. He is funny because he is, after all, the one who brought on most of his present woes. It may be galling to him to be told that his victim, Jenny Hill, is in praying for his soul. But Bill it was who made her his victim, thus giving her the chance to heap on her tormentor the proverbial coals of fire.

### Peter Shirley

Shirley, as he first appeared, was the pitiable example of social injustice. Even then, to be sure, he was not one to underplay his own miseries. He was angry and bitter. Yet his obvious near-starvation insured him some sympathy, and his brave retorts to the menacing Bill roused admiration. There is, however, a vindictive streak in him. He seems rather to enjoy watching the younger man squirm and to relish the prospect of his being ruined by gin, trounced by Todger, or arrested by Barbara. This sort of development of Shirley's character is quite in keeping with Shaw's over-all thesis. Shaw's target for attack in this play is poverty in general, which he will have Undershaft characterize as a "crime." To build up this concept he will first work up some dismay over Shirley's suffering.

A system that so discards willing workers cannot be an ideal one. Then he has Shirley defy Walker. In this incident Shirley shows for an instant the fiery, proud spirit of a human being with dignity rather than the crushed subservience of the starving pauper. But, notably, it is only for a minute. Let Walker merely remind him of his desolate condition, and Shirley bursts into tears of grief and frustration. Thus in a few brief exchanges Shirley has served to demonstrate first, the kind of mettlesome human being he might be had he not been hobbled by an inequitable system, and second, the pitiable wreck he has become.

Yet both Shirley's misery and Shirley's defiance are likely to win audience sympathy for the man. And Shaw is not one to put much stress upon the personal nobility of the poor. He has already in the characters of Rummy and Snobby launched a telling attack upon the sentimentalist's conception of the poor as humble, grateful, and beatifically consoled by religion. His thinking is that poverty is a monstrous evil and that the more stress is laid upon the goodness and spiritual strength of the destitute, the less is going to be done to remedy the whole situation.

Hence, he does not show even Shirley as altogether attractive. Having worked all his life, Shirley has at this point more self-respect and independence than those perennial recipients of charity, Rummy and Snobby. He still sometimes talks and acts like a real man. But already his lot has made him mean and embittered. Having been superseded by younger men, he acts with even greater vindictiveness toward Walker. And he positively gloats over the possibility that Todger may give him a beating. To sum up, if Shirley or any of the other poor people are shown to have remained assured, dignified, and generally estimable, then Shaw sacrifices some of his argument that poverty is a blight that destroys those whom it hits. Here Shirley is beginning to develop the mean, whining spirit that Shaw associates with the class who suffer constantly from humiliating deprivation.

## SIGNIFICANT THEMES

### Evils Of Poverty

Despite Barbara's kindly attempt to be matter-of-fact and tactful, Shirley obviously finds distasteful even the necessary questions as to his age and qualifications. And the query as to his religion causes him to bridle instantly. Except for the twinges of conscience that put him at some disadvantage, Bill Walker can be much more lofty and even insolent. But Shirley is trapped, bewildered, and inclined to be resentful.

### The Workings Of Conscience

There will be more about guilt and conscience as the play proceeds. Up to now the unruly Bill has been duly impressed with the threats of such consequences of his action as a beating or imprisonment. Yet those are external, comprehensible penalties that he could accept if necessary, and eventually even shrug off as part of the game. But the word that the inoffensive and abused Jenny Hill is praying for him, he finds every bit as alarming as Barbara probably intends. And he is even more upset when she suggests that God, through his own personal conscience, will torment him for his deed until he repents and accepts salvation. Bill's one hope for escape from this terrifying idea is to get away from the shelter, go to Canningtown and retrieve Mog, first beating up her new "bloke." This, he feels, will restore his sense of self-satisfaction. But Barbara first informs him that Mog has changed - no longer sluttish, she has washed her hair and has a new sense of joy. And she is now loved by Todger, who can easily knock him down. Bill thus sees his sole opportunity to stifle conscience cut off by Barbara. "She's dan me." he says despairingly. In this play Shaw will take a stand against the usual punishments imposed by society, such as imprisonment, on the grounds that they are cruel and unavailing. He believes instead that the conscience must be roused and so impressed with the irrevocable and inexpiable nature of the offense that it will never want again to undergo the same remorse. Even at this point, Bill is beginning to wish that he had never seen Jenny Hill, although no one has obviously "punished" him in any way but talk.

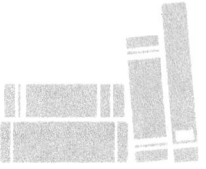

# MAJOR BARBARA

## TEXTUAL ANALYSIS

## ACT 2, SCENES 5-7

### ACT II, SCENE 5

#### SUMMARY

Barbara summons the wounded Jenny, whose sweet forgiving attitude agonizes Bill further. Undershaft arrives and Barbara tells Shirley he is a Secularist. Her father corrects her. He is a mystic; his religion is being a Millionaire. He then snorts at Shirley's self-righteous pride. Sending Rummy and Shirley in to wash dishes, Barbara goes on gently but implacably badgering Bill. She almost defeats him, but then Cusins arrives. No longer hypnotized, Bill warns Dolly to check his fiance or face a difficult life. He then exits in search of a solacing retributory blow from Todger, as Cusins ponders.

## Comment

Barbara's haughty assurance is most apparent in this scene. She calls Jenny out for the express purpose of deepening Bill's remorse and almost peremptorily orders Shirley and Rummy in to help with the work in the shelter. She is also coolly certain of herself as she demonstrates to her father how to stir up a man's conscience. Yet with the arrival of both Undershaft and Cusins, she will henceforth tend to lose command of the operation. Undershaft has contradicted her as to his religion. Shirley responds with some bitterness. And Bill, whom she had almost downed completely, suddenly gets a new view of her as a young engaged woman. Barbara has introduced Cusins as her "bloke" to establish relations on a friendly basis of relative equality. But in so doing, she seems to sacrifice a measure of the awesome remoteness that had impressed Bill against his will. Major Barbara, granddaughter of an Earl and imperious in her own right, is a strong, even awesome antagonist. But Barbara as daughter and prospective bride begins to lose subtly some of her dominating force. Although the play is called *Major Barbara*, Shaw is said to have considered entitling it "Andrew Undershaft's Profession," thus continuing the curious series hitherto including his Mrs. Warren's Profession and Cashel Byron's Profession. Although he did not go ahead with his plan, he very definitely gives Undershaft the most provocative and serious ideas to advance. And from this point on, it is Undershaft and not his daughter, who will clearly be the character in command.

BRIGHT NOTES STUDY GUIDE

## CHARACTER ANALYSIS

### Barbara Undershaft

In this scene Barbara is cool, poised, good natured, and again fiercely determined. Simply and passionately convinced that she has found "salvation" and both can and should impart it to others, she is able to pursue Bill with an almost terrifying zeal. She is the strong-willed daughter of two imperious parents, and according to the stage directions her resemblance to her mother especially is supposed to be brought out by the actress playing the scene. Again, those who know *Man and Superman* will see her running down her spiritual quarry with the same awesome directness that Ann employs to wear down the marital resistance of the confirmed bachelor, John Tanner. For Ann's uncompromising and even unscrupulous tactics, Shaw has his own philosophical explanation. She is cooperating in her own instinctive fashion with the "Life-Force," by trying to obtain for herself a superior father for the children she is destined to bear. This will not here apply to Barbara although she is equally set upon imposing her will upon a man. She is in love with Cusins, not Bill. But Shaw clearly has carried over certain traits from his earlier "Life-Force" characterizations.

There is, however, a further possibility. To look ahead, Shaw is going eventually to have Barbara withdraw from the Army because its methods are less effectual than the frankly profit-conscious Undershaft's in raising the level of society. Hence, when Barbara and her workers are trying to "save" Rummy, Snobby, and even Peter with bread and treacle and thinned milk, they are merely bolstering an inequitable system. Bill Walker, however, is no recipient of Army charity as such. In rousing his conscience and refusing to let him regard his offense lightly or atone for it perfunctorily, Barbara is not supporting any current form of false thinking. Here, in Shaw's view, she is clearly on the side of human progress and is thus, in a different way, working in harmony with that "Life-Force," that would from generation to generation improve the race.

## Andrew Undershaft

When the munitions maker agreed to come to the shelter, he first drove a bargain. Barbara could try to convert him to her way of thinking, but then he would have the chance to counter with his views at the factory on the following day. Actually, he comes prepared to do battle even in West Ham and will set about systematically wrecking Barbara's confident assumptions practically from the moment he arrives. As good-humored and pleasant, generally, as Barbara is with Bill, he may disarmingly suggest the indulgent father. But Undershaft is always keen, alert, and purposive. His active mind may enjoy a bit of intellectual give and take. But he is wilier and more experienced than the bright but overconfident Barbara. And not for nothing has the shrewd enough Lady Britomart described him as one of the most feared men in Europe.

Is Undershaft then hero or villain? He is about to take a somewhat unfair advantage, afforded him by money, position, and unusual acumen, and destroy something that gave his appealing daughter a great deal of satisfaction. Even the sardonic Cusins will suggest that there is something devilish about him. This question has caused some debate among critics, and judgments have varied, to some extent depending upon the values held by different individuals. For instance, one who thinks highly of the efforts of the Salvation Army and is not at all impressed with the ruthless armament czar's "mystic" faith of being a "Millionaire," will have difficulty envisioning him as hero. But Shaw has a fairly definite set of standards here, and in terms of what the play-wright regards as desirable, Undershaft is not particularly reprehensible. Indeed, if he has any fatherly feelings for Barbara and if he wants what is best for her, he must make every effort to "educate" her as to how best she can put to use her obviously superior gifts. The "education" may, unfortunately, cause some heartbreak. But this is the price that may have to be paid for her genuine spiritual progress.

Undershaft here affirms that he is no "Secularist," but a mystic with a religion, that of being a "Millionaire." In the previous Act, he had told his wife that religion, far from being a disagreeable subject, was the only one in which capable people were really interested. He had, in addition, indicated to Lomax that his religion was unconventional or unorthodox. For him it was a true religion, but it was that especially of a maker of armaments. This mysticism of Undershaft's will be explained further in subsequent scenes. In general, however, Shaw means here by a religion, first of all, a strong and meaningful set of values that form the basis of an intelligent man's thoughts and actions. Lady Britomart has talked of Undershaft's "religion of wrongness." But essentially, Shaw is glancing at those of his contemporaries who call themselves Christians but either ignore their faith in actual practice or so engage in rationalizations that they make a mockery of affirmed principles. Undershaft, by contrast, has developed his own satisfying life standards, admits them openly ("Unashamed"), and follows them consistently. One definition of religion is "any specific system of belief, worship, conduct, etc., often involving a code of ethics and a philosophy" (*Webster's New World Dictionary of the American Language*, 1960 ed., p. 1228). In this sense, regardless of his attitudes toward the supernatural, Undershaft certainly has a religion.

But a "mystic" is something else again. Although the customary concept of a mystic has suggested those saintly individuals granted special glimpses of matters heavenly, the term may also include those who understand by intuition truths beyond the ken of ordinary mortals. Later in the play Undershaft will suggest that whereas his immediate personal objective is to increase his own profits (a Millionaire, by religious conviction), he still feels that he is being used by some power or force to advance civilization. Again here there will be Shaw's idea of the mysterious but basic "Life-Force" always aiming at a higher development of the human race. Some human beings cooperate with it more fully and thus make that development actually perceivable. Undershaft through his operation not only does contribute to this progress, but also, being unusually intelligent or possibly intuitive, realizes that he is being used as part of some vast admirable design. And it is in this awareness that his "mysticism" largely consists. It must be remembered that Charles Darwin and other thinkers during the half-century before Shaw wrote *Major Barbara* had been working out various theories of evolution, according to which the human race as well as other forms of life under-went certain progressive changes over the centuries. Shaw was what is sometimes called an "eclectic" thinker. He did not take over exactly the theory of anyone scientist or philosopher but chose certain ideas from various systems and out of them constructed his own. Yet it is certainly apparent that Shaw like many others of his era was thinking more or less in evolutionary terms.

One other comment by Undershaft is worth noting here. The industrialist quite sharply takes issue with Shirley when the latter declares that he is poor and "proud of it." He declares in opposition that no one has cause to be proud of poverty and snorts at Shirley's suggestion that at least the poor man has a superior "conscience." At first glance, these remarks by Barbara's father may seem to be in poor taste, to say the least. Here the man with millions, with power, prestige, and every luxury at his command, would seem to be rather cruelly lording it over the impoverished workman who has literally nothing save perhaps some vestiges of self-respect. Barbara may be unconsciously a trifle patronizing, but she does try to be tactful. But here the arch capitalist gravely yet unmistakably sneers at the pauper. In other writings of the era this might not be surprising. Karl Marx and others had begun to launch bitter attacks upon the capitalist system, and there would with fair frequency be representations of proud, cruel, selfish, hateful rich men. Shaw, however, has not up to now portrayed Undershaft as an obvious villain. He has shown him rather as a genial older man, generous enough to his family despite an international reputation for being formidable. So how should this retort to Shirley be interpreted?

One of Shaw's main concerns in this play is with poverty as such. He believes that for too long people have accepted the existence of a large number of poor people in any society as inevitable, and as a result have done little to eliminate the miseries entailed. Furthermore, he is convinced that certain attitudes and conventional measures adopted over the ages by monied or well-to-do groups have helped even further to perpetuate such evils. One such, to him, is the myth of the noble poor man. We have seen that up to now in his representations of Rummy, Snobby, Shirley, and Walker, he has shown far from wholly admirable members of the humbler classes. Above all he would break down the notion that poverty, in itself, is necessarily virtuous. For if it is in some way good or noble, why try to eliminate it? So long, the argument runs, as the Shirleys are for any reason proud of being poor, the longer it may take them to force whatever changes are necessary to get them a fair share of the over-all wealth. Thus, were Undershaft more "tactful," were he to soothe and flatter the poor man into settling for his consciousness of being righteous instead of seeking to get his share, Undershaft in Shaw's view would be truly villainous. When, on the other hand, he sharply challenges the poor man's smug assumptions, he is in reality helping him get a true picture, one that may spur him on to stop whining, stop begging for charity rations, and start fighting his way up toward prosperity. This was what Undershaft, initially a poor foundling, did. Now, in effect, he calls Shirley to do likewise.

## Bill Walker

Here Walker, for all his efforts to remain independent and cocky, is given a hard time by the zealous, relentless Barbara. She is more articulate and more quick-thinking than he is, and, as she claims, she has undoubtedly had considerable experience with similar cases. In addition, she is a dynamic personality, something of a spell-binder. And, what is a more, Bill is sensitive enough so that his own conscience helps leave him vulnerable. He is not, of course, under arrest. Nothing but his own troubled spirit keeps him at the shelter to listen to Barbara's infuriating attempts to "save" him. At this point, however, further dismayed by the sight of the bandaged Jenny with her sweetly forgiving smile, Bill is ashamed and a little frightened. Barbara has thoroughly alarmed him by further hinting that the uncomfortable feelings of remorse that he now experiences are not going to pass away easily, but are going to continue pricking him whatever he does. However he may attempt his old swaggering manner, Bill cannot shake off the dismal suspicion that she may know whereof she speaks. So his problem is how to free himself from this sudden and appalling manifestation of guilt and shame. For a time he hesitates, not having any ready solution. And the longer he stays, the more Barbara works to accentuate his interior turmoil. And she almost wins. In her preaching of "salvation," she at least seems to offer some way of escape, and he is growing desperate. Moreover, her firm, persuasive manner exerts an almost hypnotic influence.

Here, the playwright himself breaks up Barbara's operation by having Adolphus Cusins come in with his big, noisy drum. This is an interesting and deliberate move on Shaw's part. For his own intellectual as well as dramatic purposes, he wants Walker's conscience thoroughly roused. Walker has acted like a drunken brute, and he would have his thoughts and feelings so stirred up that he begins to reach toward a higher level of human experience. But one thing Shaw does not want. He does not intend that all of Walker's new man-sized dilemmas will be neatly and gloriously solved by his "conversion" to Barbara's Salvation Army faith. He has other, and to him better, plans for Walker. The play, it must be realized, is not an out-and-out attack upon the Army. The Army has faith, enthusiasm, and a positive spirit. It does something to help people and perhaps serves a temporary need. Without it, presumably, Shirley starves. But its basic answers are not those advocated by Shaw. So Bill is cleverly snatched out of the well-meaning Barbara's clutches just as he seems about to yield to her highly efficient salesmanship.

In the lines that follow, Bill serves two purposes. First of all, there is, after the serious conversion attempt, an easing-off into more conventional comedy. Suddenly seeing Barbara, the oracular priestess, in a new light, that of a girl engaged to a "bloke," Bill becomes again almost jocular. Allying himself with all exasperated males, he solicitously warns Cusins to assert whatever authority he can muster before it is too late. In addition, he prepares the way for further Shaw discussion as to the nature of guilt and the role of punishment or atonement. For he announces that he is going to Canningtown to get himself beaten by the stronger and heavier Todger Fairmile so that he may be free from any further recriminations about the Jenny Hill incident. He will then be "square," once and for all. Actually, the move will not, as Barbara suggests, solve his problem at all. But this Bill cannot yet know. So he sets off, with some signs of renewed optimism.

## Peter Shirley

This scene again stresses Shirley's more negative qualities. He is quite angry when Barbara orders him rather summarily into help the volunteers wash the dishes. He had, of course, previously objected to being merely an object of charity. But he does not like being so quickly reminded of his obligations. He is, in fact, astonished when Barbara suggests that he might assist the tired lasses out of "love." Deep down, he has never had much regard for the upper classes, as is clear from his reply to Undershaft. And the idea of his being united to even those who have been his benefactors in some bond of mutual esteem seems a startling novelty.

He is also furious when Undershaft rejects his contention that he has caused to be proud, being no millionaire. He irately insists that he has made money for such as the munitions magnate and that the upper classes have kept him and the other workers poor. Hence, he implies, the poor have some claim to a good conscience, and rich men like Undershaft should be ashamed of themselves. But Undershaft's motto is "Unashamed." And the play's general line is that there is no special virtue in being poor. Noble qualities, its thesis runs, develop in favorable environments. Poverty encourages servility, hypocrisy, meanness, vindictiveness, all the baser qualities observed in the poor characters shown on the stage. It is, Undershaft will later aver, a man's duty to be as affluent as he can be. So Shirley has no cause to pride himself upon the fact that he has failed to make millions.

## SIGNIFICANT THEMES

### Evils Of Poverty

Shirley is humiliated by Barbara's command to go in and help with the cleaning. He is also urged to feel no claim to moral superiority as compared with the rich. The poor man here is thus shown to be wretched, resentful, and dependent without even the legitimately comforting assurance that he is nobler than his oppressive "betters."

### Conscience And Atonement

Barbara assures Bill that the very consciousness of his misdeed will cause him suffering no matter where he goes. She suggests that he will feel better if he accepts the Army and its "salvation." Bill, however, believes that if he can, through the pain inflicting power of Todger's fists, endure more physical anguish than his victim, Jenny, he will then be more than "square," and will again be untroubled. Shaw will not accept either solution as the play proceeds.

### TOPICS FOR DISCUSSION

Is Undershaft justified in his contention that the poor as such have no cause to feel morally superior? Does Walker's plan of atoning by taking a beating from Todger make any sense?

### ACT II, SCENE 6

#### SUMMARY

When Barbara reenters the shelter, Undershaft accuses Cusins of shamming an interest in the Army to win her. Adolphus replies that he collects religions and believes them all. Besides, the Army preaches happiness, love, and bravery, and thus spiritually elevates all, even teachers of Greek. Undershaft defines his own religion as that of money and gunpowder, since wealth and power are needed for the good life. He admires his daughter and will win her through religion. Cusins calls him mad, but Undershaft declares that he will convince Barbara by "buying" the Army. Then he, Cusins, and Barbara will stand together to help the

> common people. Returning, Barbara bemoans the poor collections since the need is so great because of widespread unemployment. She hates to be always begging, but loftily refuses her father's tainted money. Her general, Mrs. Baines, has prayed for funds, and Barbara believes some will be forthcoming. Mrs. Baines has asked, she adds in all innocence, to be introduced today to Undershaft.

## Comment

In terms of Shaw's outlining of provocative ideas, this is quite an important scene. One of its most interesting aspects is its concern with "madness." The more Undershaft sees of Barbara, the more he is convinced that in her he has found an admirable prospective missionary for his own curious religion of "money and gunpowder." As he waxes eloquent on this subject, Cusins questions his sanity, since Barbara has shown no signs whatsoever of considering her father's dedicated concern for explosives a way of life for which she will give up her work with the Army. Undershaft amiably does not deny the charge of madness, but claims that anyone like Cusins who translates such ancient Greek writers as Euripides, and anyone like Barbara who sets out to transform souls must be just as insane as he seems. According to one student of Shaw, Maurice Colbourne, it is sometimes difficult for us to decide when the playwright is talking seriously and when he is merely engaging in intellectual sport, tossing off stimulating ideas more or less for the sake of being entertaining. One reliable test. however, says Colbourne, for pinpointing the dramatist's own convictions, is to watch carefully any character in the plays whom others therein describe as mad. More than likely, he claims, the "real" Shaw is lurking in whatever speeches brought on the accusation (*The Real Bernard Shaw*, p. 87). If Colbourne is right, this would then be a passage to consider carefully.

The scene is also important because it develops earlier hints of a possible curious understanding between Barbara's father and Barbara's fiance. From the very beginning there has been a closer sympathy of some sort between the two than, say, between Undershaft and his son, Stephen. Cusins quickly and efficiently settled the mistaken identify situation when Undershaft first arrived, although, as a nice touch, Shaw had the millionaire automatically light upon Adolphus in error as the one young man out of the three who looked like a possible offspring. Cusins, too, seemed the only one, with the possible exception of Barbara, who did not bridle at once when the older man started propounding his radical ideas. Yet here Undershaft rather daringly takes Cusins into his confidence, when not shrewdly probing to discover the professor's own rather unusual convictions. To some extent, the scene thus fulfills an expository function. We know a great deal more about both of these men as it comes to a close. But this also represents, in effect, the formation of an alliance.

Undershaft and Cusins are in some ways quite different personalities. The munitions maker appears to be a strong active man of business, tough and resourceful in addition to being used to wealth, power, and influence. He seems quite naturally one to take command of any situation. By contrast, the thin, none too robust, bespectacled professor of Greek seems witty enough but somewhat, as he himself admits, ineffectual. Lady Britomart has no illusions that he is ever going to provide much material support for her daughter. And the description of him as banging a large drum around the Salvation Army shelter out of some infatuation for Barbara does not suggest a particularly forceful personality.

In this scene, however, the parallels are drawn. First of all, both men have supple, rather bold intellects and are capable of visions that go beyond the ordinary. Cusins sees the Army's religion in comparison with a variety of other types of spiritual experience and "believes" in it in a way that would baffle and annoy many of its more literal devotees. Undershaft, on his part, can dream of what seems a fantastic combination of himself, Cusins, and Barbara initiating a program for human betterment on a grand scale.

In addition, both, in their respective fashions, are ruthless opportunists. Undershaft, to no one's surprise, indicates in this scene that he intends to have his own way regardless of what measures he has to take, or whom or what he has to buy. But Cusins is equally adamant. At one point, in bringing up the somewhat ticklish question of the professor's limited financial resources, Undershaft somehow creates the impression that he might endanger Cusins' plan to marry Barbara. The younger man will have none of this. With sharp finality, he insists as politely as possible that he, too, is accustomed to getting whatever it is that he really wants. So, inasmuch as he now really wants Barbara, her father, for all his millions, had better not try to interfere. The munitions magnate, not unexpectedly, is delighted with this show of spirit, "after his own heart."

One snag, however, suggests itself. Undershaft has made no secret of his regard for "money and power." Cusins, on the contrary, indicates that he may oppose him by linking himself firmly with Barbara on the basis of their mutual love for the common people. But he makes the mistake here of referring to that love as a "romance," and that gives Undershaft his cue.

Shaw, in general, in his works opposes "romance," in the sense that it represents a false view of life. In its stead he purports to offer "realism." So here Undershaft argues that when Barbara and her fiance talk of loving the poor or of finding any blessing in poverty, they are lapsing into sentimentality. He, Cusins, is talking like a professor, and she is, after all, the sheltered granddaughter of an earl. Undershaft, by contrast, has been poor and has no such illusions. As a realist, he insists that the three must form an elite and so change conditions that in effect there will be no more poor at all. They must bring those below them now in some way up to their own level. He adds further that in order to accomplish this superior design, he will buy Barbara's Army.

This last pronouncement momentarily alienates Cusins. And this again indicates the playwright's skill. An excellent teacher of drama, William Thomas Walsh, years ago used to inform his college classes that the able stage craftsman had to employ the art of "tacking." This is a nautical term describing the type of maneuver by which a sailboat is headed now one way, now another, yet always in the general direction of the port. The playwright always has the problem of advancing his action without so settling all the vital difficulties that he has nothing left to maintain suspense until the very end of the drama. In general, Shaw is going to establish a strong bond by the last scene between Undershaft and Cusins. But he uses "tacking" in this scene. He has the two of them, already linked by a common affection for Barbara, discover that they have much more in common as personalities than they or the audience may hitherto have suspected. And they give notice to expressions of mutual admiration.

But Shaw does not want everything straightened out at once between them. So he has Undershaft go too far for even the rather dispassionate Cusins. His confident talk of getting control of the Army by money, regardless of his earlier suggestion of altruistic intent, is more than Cusins can at present accept. Before this he had called Undershaft a "rascal," and made it seem almost a term of admiration. Now he uses the same term "rascal," but with some horror. Undershaft is clearly a persuasive advocate. So given the opportunity, he might well overcome this newly roused antagonism. But Shaw, as playwright, will not let this happen, any more than he would let Barbara carry through Bill's conversion. So, just at this point, he brings onstage Barbara, Price, and Jenny to create distractions, change the subject, and, by the talk of poor collections and the arrival of Mrs. Baines, prepare for a whole new line of development. It is suggested that Shaw is mainly a playwright of ideas, not much sometimes interested in plots. And he himself once said, according to Frank Harris, "I avoid plots as I would the plague" (Bernard Shaw, p. 249). But, as is evident from a scene such as this, he does have an impressive grasp of the mechanics of scene building and does manage his stage transitions with undeniable artistry.

## CHARACTER ANALYSIS

### Andrew Undershaft

In this scene, Undershaft is at once half-cynical realist and visionary. His contention, that such virtues as "honor, justice, truth, love, mercy" and others can exist only where there is enough money and gunpowder, or wealth and power, to provide a basis, is one of the play's more controversial views. Curiously enough, Shaw has Barbara, returning weary after energetically begging for a few coins, seem partially to support this theory. How can she, she demands brokenly, talk religion to a starving man? Yet some have questioned the validity of Undershaft's rather sweeping generalization. The implication would seem to be that none of the normally considered admirable traits could exist at all among the poor, and hence that people like Snobby and Rummy would be wholly typical of the dispossessed. In so maintaining, Shaw, or at least Undershaft, is putting a tremendous stress upon the formative influence of environment. Oddly enough, the generalization does not work both ways. Both Barbara and the other two young Undershafts were presumably given the same environmental advantages. Yet Barbara became an eager, progressive worker for humanity, and the other two, like Lomax, show no signs of any enterprise whatsoever. On the other hand, Undershaft, who according to his own statement sprang from the depths of deprivation, developed somehow the initiative and the determination to forge ahead.

At the same time, as some critics have warned us, it may be useful to regard Shaw as a sort of propagandist of ideas to be taken seriously, but not necessarily literally. In the England of his time, as Barbara no doubt accurately indicates, there was a great deal of dire poverty. By 1905, charitable groups, largely religious, were trying to alleviate the misery. And there were those who felt that the government should do more to help out the unfortunate and abandon the earlier "laissez faire" or "let alone" policy that tended to favor the wealthy. The efforts made, however, had still by no means come close to eliminating the evils. So Shaw would regard it as extremely important that the public do more thinking about the problem. In general, he would seem to be sound in maintaining that an atmosphere of dirt, disease, and over-all misery is not conducive to the best development of the individual. Nothing discovered before or since his time regarding the effects of slum conditions would suggest the influences of such environments have been as a rule benign. So Shaw's general urging that environments be improved would be in line with sound social theory, regardless of the rather extreme implication that virtue cannot flourish at all under hardship conditions.

There is, nevertheless, something almost brutally cynical about Undershaft's proposal to "buy" the Army. We have seen that in connection with the play's plot structuring, this talk of Undershaft's is used to hold up the developing understanding between him and Cusins, so that the play may not lose all of its suspense. But Cusins' outraged defense of the Army's integrity is probably more acceptable to many than Undershaft's rather coldly calculating prediction. Yet Shaw's basic contention must always be kept in mind. He claims, simply enough, that the whole present system is unfair and that well-meaning charitable groups like the Salvation Army help to perpetuate it rather than correct it. Now Undershaft argues quite unanswerably that the Army cannot carry on its activities without funds. And were there any doubts as to his accuracy, there will shortly after he heard the idealistic Barbara's gloomy fears that the shelter will soon have to close despite the widespread penury that makes its operations so necessary.

In view then of the undisputed needs of the Army, Undershaft declares that he can "buy" it, presumably with a sizable donation. Here there are two points being made. Obviously, Undershaft says nothing about taking over personal direction or using the organization in some overt fashion for some curious design of his own. He does not suggest, for instance, that he intends to deluge the shelters with munitions propaganda or perhaps set up through it a private police force. Such tactics are in the realm more of the crime or spy adventure story.

What Undershaft does claim is that if the Army has his money to spread around, it will work to make the poor less discontented with their miserable lot. It will take care of their most crying needs and then through its preaching of religion keep them resigned and docile. The result will be that he will have a steady supply of sober, docile workers and no trouble whatsoever with such troublesome movements as Socialism. When he so analyzes the situation, Undershaft, to Shaw, is being merely "realistic," rather than callous. Whatever the wishful "romantic" thinking of Cusins, Undershaft is pointing out the true fact of a sorry situation. By contrast, suppose that he does not carry out his wily scheme and that he and his fellow industrial pirates do not put up the funds to "buy" the Army. Then, by inference, all such palliatives will fail, and faced with more dire prospects than ever, the deprived will rise and demand their rights, thus bringing about probably a more equitable distribution of wealth.

Undershaft, of course, has envisioned an informed and dedicated trio, himself, Barbara, and Cusins, bringing about a gradual uprising of the masses. Buying the Army will presumably give him time to accomplish his mystic purpose with the least possible inconvenience, as opposed to the possible revolutionary consequences of letting the religious organizations fail immediately. In addition, however, to make his long-range plan a reality, he must detach Barbara from the Army and align her with his specific interests. He is shrewd enough to know how disillusioned she will be if the Army, as it must to survive, accepts his check. So his move in the buying proposal has a two-fold objective. By quelling any immediate desperation moves to rebel, he will have his way clear to effect some reorganization of society at his own speed and in his own way. He will also, he believes, so open the eyes of his daughter that she will of necessity become part of his grand future designs.

Interestingly enough, in this section Cusins uses several terms to describe Undershaft. He calls him twice an "infernal" rascal and later refers to him as "Mephistopheles" and "Machiavelli." Both the "infernal" and the "Mephistopheles" suggest, of course, the traditional powers of darkness. And the critic, Arthur Nethercot, has devoted considerable space in his study of Shaw's characters to an analysis of Shaw's "diabolic" characters. Some will recall that Shaw has another play, *The*

*Devil's Disciple*, in which the title applies to the work's hero. But Nethercot calls Undershaft Shaw's "prize specimen" of this type of portrait (*Men and Supermen*, p. 63). In general, Shaw's "devil" characters are intelligent and decidedly unconventional. They are also likely to have few ordinary scruples and go after their objectives with a bold disregard for the strictures of the allegedly pious folk whom they shock. Actually, in general, just as Shaw's "mad" characters seem to be those whom he regards as truly sane, so his diabolical ones are likely to be his more advanced thinkers. To him most of the more reputedly sane and godly people, such as Lady Britomart or Lomax, are steeped in false thinking and consciously or otherwise committed to the support of thoroughly unjust customs and institutions.

As for the "Machiavelli" label, the original Florentine writer on political subjects lived from 1469 to 1527. In his famous book *The Prince*, he described the efficient methods used by unscrupulous princes to obtain and hold the reins of government. Actually his work was essentially a scientific analysis of which procedures, moral or otherwise, had proved most efficient in statecraft, in terms of recorded historical results. From Shakespeare's time on, however, the name had special connotations, especially in England. A "Machiavellian" there would be any unscrupulous individual who had a clearly defined goal, weighed carefully alternate procedures, and acted subtly and dispassionately to remove all obstacles from his path. Richard III, for instance, in Shakespeare's historical tragedy, is specifically labeled in the text a Machiavellian character. But just as Shaw's madmen may be sane and his devils in a sense angelic, so his Machiavellian may not be so villainous as the type usually suggests. Yet he will certainly be a cool, resourceful schemer, unburdened by the scruples of average men. In so describing Undershaft, Cusins here refers particularly to his plan to win over Barbara by destroying her illusions about the Army. As in the term "infernal" there probably remains even here some tantalizing aura of wickedness. But then Shaw seems never to have objected to whatever suggestion of interesting mischief-making clung to him or his heroes.

## Adolphus Cusins

When Lady Britomart accused Cusins of joining the Army merely to woo Barbara, he offered no defense. When, however, her husband makes the same charge, he claims to be a collector of religions and to "believe" in the way that he believes in the others. Here, in all probability, the attitude of Cusins reflects fairly accurately that of Shaw. The playwright had no Barbara to court, but he, too, seems to have found certain aspects of the Army's work commendable. For instance, Cusins refers specifically to the joyous sound of its lively music. And Shaw, the music critic and enthusiast, had offered on one occasion a spirited defense of the Army's bands.

In addition, Cusins lauds the positive spirit of the Army, in that it stresses joy, love, and courage. What Shaw and Cusins objected to most strongly was the gloomier side of some more conventional religious observances. In a passage with ironic import, Lady Britomart rebuked Barbara for treating religion as a "pleasant" matter. And Cusins, in bowing out of family prayers, cited the, to him, objectionable passages proclaiming one's guilt. Furthermore, the Army was, as Cusins points out, justifying itself pragmatically, that is, by results. By rescuing some men and women from heavy drinking and other debilitating vices, it was helping a few at least to achieve the sort of human dignity that Shaw wanted for all. So compared with some of the older, less "progressive" and less heartily cheerful faiths, the Salvation Army was commendable. He does not see it, however, as the most satisfying solution since it fails to get to the root of the whole problem, which is the uneven distribution of wealth under capitalism.

Cusins is also, of course, identified as a professor of Greek, and here he cites rather freely certain poetic passages from the Greek playwright, Euripides. As mentioned previously, Cusins is said to have been based upon the classical scholar, Gilbert Murray, whom Shaw much admired. In quoting Euripides, Cusin admits that the translation may not be wholly accurate. Actually, Shaw seems to have adapted certain Murray translations in a way that would suit his own dramatic purposes. Apart from developing the professional aspect of Barbara's fiance, the poetic lines sum up Cusins' belief that apart from Undershaft's money and guns, there is a certain joy in merely being alive and being able to appreciate beauty, to him epitomized in Barbara. Undershaft, however, sardonically brings up at once the matter of the professor's income, again driving home his thesis that without wealth and power no other elements of the good life are normally possible. Joy and love, or aesthetic satisfactions, are merely to Undershaft those "graces and luxuries" that can be afforded only when economic security has been attained. In his monumental work on Shaw, Gilbert K. Chesterton argues that Shaw, who usually gives the opponents in his onstage debates fairly good cases to present, grants his classics teacher no telling arguments at all and allows him thus to be too readily overcome by the munitions czar (George Bernard Shaw, pp. 170–171). The explanation would seem to be that *Major Barbara* is intended to convey some of Shaw's more serious convictions, rather than to give various theories equal opportunity to beguile. His object in allying Undershaft, Barbara, and Cusins would appear to be to combine the cultivated mind of the scholar, the love and enthusiasm of the missionary, and the power, wealth, and organizing skills of the successful and enlightened capitalist to effect the needed transformation of the whole society. When concerned with so comprehensive a vision, he is no more disposed that Undershaft himself to be fair to the opposition. Cusins will thus be given just enough of a "case" to enable Undershaft to dispose of objections and eventually see that the young man fits in well with him impressive designs for the future.

## Barbara Undershaft

Four traits of Barbara are developed here for the furthering of Shaw's plot and Undershaft's plan. First of all, she is shown to be tired and very humanly discouraged. Where she triumphantly carrying all before her, she might be more able to withstand her father's carefully planned assault upon her beliefs. Secondly, she is a confirmed idealist, refusing with airy contempt her father's offer of a contribution. Interestingly enough, she rejects his money on the grounds that it has been gained in an immoral business and therefore cannot be used to purchase his "salvation." To be sure, he never in any way suggests that he is in the least interested in saving his soul through such a gesture. But Barbara is accustomed to thinking exclusively in such terms. And admittedly, the previous day's bargain between them had centered upon the question of conversion. For his part, of course, regardless of the misapprehension involved, Undershaft has no objection to her concentration on this point, since it helps lay the groundwork for the main attack which is to follow.

Thirdly, Barbara, like her mother, has excellent recuperative powers. The scene will be recalled in which Lady Britomart gives way to tears of frustration, only to brush off quickly Stephen's offer of consolation. Here Barbara, momentarily downhearted, similarly cuts short the comforting ministrations of Jenny Hill. When she will later suffer a more serious setback, Barbara may not recover quite so easily. But, as her father can see, recover she will.

Finally, she is almost incredibly naive. After loudly proclaiming the shelter's desperate need for money, she announces that her general, Mrs. Baines, has asked to meet Undershaft, but cannot imagine why. Here, perhaps, the playwright is rather obviously pulling the strings, for Barbara all along has been credited with a lively intelligence, and the subject of money has been uppermost in everyone's mind. But where she to suspect that Mrs. Baines will seek from Undershaft the contributions Barbara has loftily declined, the subsequent psychic blow would be far less shattering. So Barbara's guileless simplicity must be stressed.

## SIGNIFICANT THEMES

### Wealth And Power

Undershaft stresses the idea that only if there is a sufficiency of money and force can all the virtues and other components of the good life, such as joy, love, and the delight in beauty, ever successfully flourish.

### Evils Of Poverty

Undershaft rebukes Cusins for suggesting that there is anything to be said in favor of dirt, disease and all the other attendant miseries that constitute the "blessings" of poverty.

### Realism Vs. Romanticism

In referring to his love for the common people, Cusins is a romantic. Undershaft, who has actually been poor, is the realist who wants only to abolish poverty entirely.

### Madness

Undershaft as a man of extraordinary vision, Cusins as a classical scholar, and Barbara as an ardent missionary are all "mad" in some favorable context, In other words, they do not follow the ordinary, uninspired precedents of the conventionally "sane."

### Salvation

Barbara rejects her father's contribution because salvation cannot be bought. Much depends, of course, here upon the varying definitions of salvation. To Undershaft it means a life with dignity and independence. And since to him this cannot be had without money, in a sense it may have to be "bought." Barbara, however, thinks in terms of a regeneration of soul that cannot be paid for with a check. Shaw will have use for this idea also in a later scene.

### ACT 2, SCENE 7

#### SUMMARY

Bill returns from Canningtown, having been benevolently floored by the powerful Todger, then prayed over by him and Mog, to the crowd's delight. Amusedly, Barbara still refuses to let him "pay" for his blow to Jenny with his one saved pound. She wants his soul. Irked with this Christian forgiveness, Bill flings down the pound and later Snobby steals it. Mrs. Baines arrives to announce a princely donation from Bodger, the whiskey distiller, and to plead for a matching one from Undershaft. He agrees, and Mrs. Baines sees heaven putting bad money to good use. Besides, there will be fewer riots to menace rich gentlemen. Barbara, having turned down poor Bill's pound, is appalled. Bodger's whiskey helps destroy the poor. How can he win salvation with a mere check? Bill laughs cynically at her discomfiture.

## Comment

This is a lively scene in which a combination of cross purposes makes for interesting conflicts of wills, Bill Walker, for instance, wants merely to dislodge the burden of guilt from his conscience. So long as he has some chance to fight back, he can keep up his morale. When the sharp-tongued Rummy Mitchens threatens him with the law, he can roar right back at her. But gentle Jenny Hill insists upon forgiving him like a Christian, and having no adequate reply, he feels ashamed and miserable. So his single idea is to give her his one precious pound and then forget the whole business.

For her part, Jenny, who is younger and less perceptive than Barbara, has three objectives. She wants, first of all, to be a sincere and consistent Christian. So she must, from her heart, forgive her enemies. In addition, she really seems to be a kind-hearted girl. So she wants to make Bill feel less ashamed of having struck her. She therefore keeps assuring him bravely that he did not hurt her much at all, even though it is obvious that he did. And her simple, dogged attempts to cheer him up succeed, naturally, only in making him feel worse. Finally, being admirably unselfish, she eyes his proffered money with some favor. Perhaps he would like to give a few coins to poor old Rummy Mitchens, whom he also struck. This seems to Bill a dreadful notion, since Rummy, the unforgiving, is not all on his conscience. Jenny then thinks that some of his money might help out others at the shelter. But this suggestion Barbara vetos.

Both ardent, idealistic, and selfless, Barbara and Jenny appear at times to be pursuing different immediate goals, although Barbara, as a true daughter of Undershaft, ably uses Jenny to serve her own spiritual purposes in regard to Bill. In effect, the more Jenny offers sweet, loving forgiveness, meant to ease remorse and quell anxieties, the more Barbara blocks all attempts to give Bill a relatively painless release. She laughs at his efforts to get himself a retributory trouncing and resolutely refuses his bribe money. At the same time, she is shrewdly aware that Jenny's unfeigned charitableness goads Bill further and so is more than willing to have Jenny forgive while she herself holds out.

The fourth figures, Mrs. Baines, has her own objectives, too. Apparently a well-intentioned, good-hearted woman, she has one basic concern-to get enough money to keep the Army shelters going; and she is not going to look too carefully or critically into the mouth of gift horses. She will use whatever funds she can raise to help care for the poor. And should the money originally have been made in rather dubious trades, it will now, by heaven's will, be purified by at least being made to serve worthy purposes.

Actually, of course, Mrs. Baines does not have to "sell" at all in order to get a donation from Undershaftd As the audience so well knows, having heard him outline his plan to Cusins, he is merely awaiting eagerly such an opportunity, for he knows that his contribution will eventually free Barbara for his great design. But ironically, of course, poor Mrs. Baines does not know what he intends. So, probably from a sort of desperation, she tries to think of arguments that will be most likely to persuade him. This gives the puppet-master, Shaw, one more chance to stress a favorite theory, already outlined by Undershaft. In times of general hardship, there is likely to be unrest among the poor. Mrs. Baines cites the riots of 1886. If, however, the rich support the Army, the worst sufferings will be alleviated and the preaching of a religion of love will discourage any violent outbreaks. In short, as Undershaft has already cynically maintained, the Army will "draw the teeth" of those with great reason to complain. Shaw himself, to be sure, is hardly in favor of widespread starvation. His attack all along has been on poverty in general. But he also is opposed to whatever drugs the populace into passively accepting evils that should be steadily and uncompromisingly opposed.

In any event, the opposing points of view here are cleverly advanced. Mrs. Baines in effect asks Undershaft to contribute to the Army for mainly selfish reasons. His check will discourage those riots that may break the windows of his club. She also is probably not unaware of the competitive sense that may make one wealthy man try to match or outdo another in generosity. When, however, Undershaft agrees, Mrs. Baines happily assures him that he is a "good" man.

Undershaft, the Machiavellian schemer, has his own game to play. To accentuate the ironies, it may be recalled that at the outset he announced to his family that unlike other industrialists he was not ashamed of his trade. He was not guilty of denying indeed the religion whose precepts he professed to believe.

Having reconciled his "religion" with his way of life, he felt no need to atone and could put his money into research rather than into hospitals, churches, or, by inference, such projects as those of the Salvation Army. And this, of course, adds satiric point to Undershaft's gleeful reminders that the whiskey distiller Bodger has not only given money to the Army but has restored a cathedral and given half a million to his political party, thus assuring himself of the title of baron. So any notion that Undershaft is contributing (as Bill offers his pound) to salve his conscience is absurd. As Barbara should realize, Undershaft is forever "Unashamed."

He has, however, admitted to Cusins that the Army in keeping the working classes sober, steady, and docile makes his work of heaping up more millions somewhat easier. So he may, as Mrs. Baines suggests, get some return for his money. But there has been no suggestion that the armaments magnate is really particularly worried about popular uprisings. His boast was that he never made contributions, and he is certainly not alarmed now. His purpose then in writing his check is primarily to "educate" his daughter and thus woo her away from the Army. This, to him, is worth a mere five thousand any day. Should the simple-hearted Mrs. Baines suspect this, would she still call him a "good" man? Probably not. Cusins' adjective "infernal" might well seem more apt. But Shaw, for his part, seems to view Undershaft's over-all plan in a fairly favorable light. Hence, to him the descriptive modifier "good," if properly interpreted, might very well seem deserved.

To sum up, then, in this admirably constructed scene, Jenny wants to soothe Bill and Barbara wants to keep him off balance. Mrs. Baines works to save the Army and Barbara to preserve its integrity. Undershaft moves to contribute generously but hopes thereby to separate from the Army one of its most able and dedicated adherents. As one final humorous but telling touch, Mrs. Baines exhibits the spuriously pious Snobby as an example of the good work accomplished by the Army. In addition to lying shamelessly, Snobby is at the moment busily filching Walker's conscience offering and running in terror from his mother who has heard of his fantastic confession of having beaten her. Here Shaw, once again, is clearly stacking cards against the Army. But this is still completely in accord with his view that this type of charity to the unfortunate clearly encourages such hypocritical displays. Even Barbara, as honest and sensible as they come, has admitted that Snobby's dramatic confession was useful in raising funds and that had he described one more sinful blow, the take would have been even better. Barbara would never herself stoop to subterfuge, but a Snobby would take the hint.

## CHARACTER ANALYSIS

### Barbara Undershaft

In the first part of the scene Barbara's mood lightens. Her interchanges with the still crestfallen Bill are in almost a gay, jocular vein. Unlike the tender-hearted Jenny, who is sympathetic when Bill tells of being held down and knelt upon by the obviously gleeful wrestler, Barbara is vastly amused. And as she blithely refuses Bill's money, it is as if she knew that victory was in the offing. There has been established a curiously amiable relationship now between the bully and this avenging angel. Although he still sputters and protests and defiantly flings down his pound, a great deal of money for a poor man, he does not run away. It is as though he were virtually on the point of surrender and were now going merely through the forms of sullen protest. Certainly, this is Barbara's feeling and she is subtly elated. In terms of the plot, she is thus actually riding for an inevitable fall.

Thanks to her wily father and the unsuspecting Mrs. Baines, the net of disillusionment is being tightened around her. But while arguing with Bill, the Major is in fine form.

As for Bill's or her father's money, Barbara will accept neither because in so doing she would be "selling" in the sense of "betraying" the Army. She refers in fact to thirty pieces of silver. She thus ties in their offer with the Bible account of the traitorous disciple, Judas, who delivered his Master, Christ, to enemies for that amount. As before, her thinking about Bill is more readily explained than her assumptions about her father. Bill clearly is trying to buy peace of soul through an atonement offering. But Undershaft actually has made no such even implied avowal. He has only sardonically offered her money to "do a great deal of good," although he has also indicated a kindly interest in solacing Bill's soul. Not once, however, has he said anything to Barbara about buying salvation with his money.

She, however, has three different ideas that motivate her refusal. In the first place, she seriously wants to save his soul. And her earlier speeches about children of one Father, sinners and salvation, plus her demonstration as regards Bill give clear evidence how she hopes to achieve her object. Briefly, her father must somehow be made to feel the pricks of conscience and the need for redeeming love. He must not be allowed a "quiet moment" until he can no longer stand out against salvation. Todger Fairmile "wrestled" with salvation, Bill is struggling, and so must Undershaft. Her only chance is to break his serene composure. For it is apparent that so long as he remains "unashamed" of his death-dealing enterprises and has nothing to work out, he will never see what Barbara calls the light. So in turning down his money, she is attempting rather naively to make him see how the saved would look upon such tainted lucre so that his conscience may be roused as was Bill's.

Secondly, she wants him to recognize and appreciate the Army's impartiality. As his daughter, she calls him "papa" and treats him with some affection. But so far as the business of the Army is concerned, she wants above all to avoid giving him or anyone else the impression that as a rich and powerful man he has any special privileges. She admits to Mrs. Baines that her position is difficult. After all, her father can remember her childhood and may never regard her as a missionary worth hearing. Yet not only for his sake but for those of her other present and prospective converts, she must treat him as one more visitor at the shelter whose state of soul must be carefully weighed before money will be accepted. True, he has not carefully outlined his intent. But Barbara is instinctively wary. Is there some ulterior motive? Even if he is not trying to buy salvation, has he something else in mind that may make all the other poor souls there highly skeptical should his donation be accepted without question?

Finally, Barbara has a certain idealistic approach to the whole operation of the Army. Clearly, she wants it never to be called in any way a tool of the rich, regardless of how they make their money. Instead she wants to be sure that all concerned with its activities are sincere believers whose contributions represent part of their "good" wealth, acquired by strictly righteous means. In short, she simply wants no connection whatsoever between the Army and the unregenerate, no matter how many extra profits they have cynically to bestow. In her own way she is holding out for a consistency of belief and practice that will keep the Army too "unashamed."

Incidentally, Shaw has in other plays dealt with this matter of the moral or immoral source of wealth. In Mrs. Warren's profession, for instance, the young Vivie is horrified to learn that she has been supported all her life by the profits from her mother's lucrative chain of houses of prostitution. And in the earlier Widowers' Houses, distress is caused to a youthful pair when they discover that their incomes have derived from rents paid for wretched slum tenements. Under Shaw's socialism, presumably, there would be efforts to eliminate such questionable enterprises.

## Andrew Undershaft

Having revealed his objective to Cusins, Barbara's father here quietly moves in for the kill. He again genially offers Barbara money, with just the right touch of carefree good humor. And when Mrs. Baines appears, he is a model of respectful courtesy. With her so intent upon her sales talk, his ambiguous compliments are accepted at face value. But the audience and the watchful Cusins can derive wry amusement watching him play the part of the suavely benevolent patron of good works. Actually, he gives out his line of pious murmurings in a way that suspiciously echoes, in cultivated fashion, the avowals of Snobby Price. By contrast, Barbara and Bill Walker are refreshing plain-spoken.

## Bill Walker

Although still serving to develop Shaw's ideas about conscience, Bill Walker here is more than ever a comic figure. His rueful account of his humiliating meeting with the two enthusiastic converts, Todger and Mog, is undeniably funny, especially since Shaw clearly suggests that the two got a great deal of dubious pious elation out of flattening poor Bill and then praying over him.

Yet being still disturbed by Barbara's claim that his only relief from the pangs of conscience will lie in his acceptance of salvation, he comes to buy his release with a pound. At that time the English pound would be worth well over five dollars and represent a large sum for men like Bill to offer. He himself regards it as a fine comparable to that imposed by the law upon a friend of his who had struck the girl he was planning to marry. As Bill explains it, his friend was entitled to beat up his fiance but Bill had no such right as regards Jenny. So he feels that it is only just that he should pay a little more.

Apart from the amusing notion about an engaged man's special privileges, the passage is interesting in that it brings in the matter of legal penalties. Barbara has been talking against the idea of accepting a voluntary contribution to soothe someone's conscience. Shaw was equally against such legal penalties as fines and imprisonment, feeling that, as Barbara maintains, "two black eyes won't make a white one" and also that the offender may conclude that having "paid his debt," he is now free to go on repeating the offense. It may be recalled that Bill has no compunction whatsoever about having hit the old and weak Rummy Mitchens. She has threatened him with the law. And law penalties, while a nuisance, are not awesome. After a man pays his fine or serves his sentence, the slate is clean. This attitude however, is precisely what Shaw would condemn. His idea is that if the conscience can be more effectively stirred, then there will be less chance that the offense will be repeated again and again.

### Mrs. Baines

The Salvation Army Commissioner is a serious older woman very much concerned about money. She is an executive, an administrator, determined to raise the money needed to keep the shelters open. Having come to the conclusion that her best solution is to solicit contributions from those who can well afford them, she has carefully worked up the arguments best calculated to persuade men hard-headed enough not to part with their wealth too readily. Her first approach is quite definitely to their own selfish interests. If the Army cares for the poor, there will be no riots to disturb them in their comfortable clubs. And they will not have to face surly, bitter men, after the Army has successfully preached its message of brotherhood. After this she will try an emotional appeal to the benevolent feelings of the fortunate. She is sincerely pious. She thanks God for all gifts and hopes that the donors will be blessed by heaven. But first and foremost, she is practical. Her organization needs cash, and she is not going to encourage any foolish scruples as to the source whence comes the necessary aid. Barbara, it may be noted, goes out of her way to be sure that any money offered comes from unimpeachable capital and is given with the purest of spiritual motives. But then Barbara, the sheltered granddaughter of an Earl, knows little about the role of wealth in her society. Like her brother, Stephen, she is going to be deeply shocked when she realizes how much she owes to the financial support provided for her from the time of her birth by Undershaft munitions. Mrs. Baines, however, knows exactly what kind of industries will furnish her contributions. And far from worrying about somewhat dubious motivations, she herself launches the appeal on a basis of strictly selfish advantage.

Throughout the play Shaw contrasts the "romantic" and the "realistic," almost always favoring the latter. Here, however, the situation is complex. Both Mrs. Baines and Undershaft are certainly realistic in realizing that the Army cannot continue its work without financial aid. And even Barbara has been forced to admit that the miserable pittance she can raise by begging her heart out on street corners will never keep the shelters from closing. Mrs. Baines is also realistic, apparently, in perceiving the reasons that are most likely to motivate ruthless captains of industry. Undershaft has anticipated her in pointing out to

Cusins that as a businessman whose primary concern is profits, he can see the advantage of supporting an organization that will draw the teeth of the poor.

In this dispute Barbara would seem to be "romantic," in that she is shying away from some of the harsher facts of a capitalistic society. Yet in her own way she has a strongly realistic streak. Committed to a strict religious code, she believes that it should be upheld consistently or not at all. She is, in effect, too "realistic" to accept the compromises adopted by Mrs. Baines to insure her organization's survival even on unsatisfactory terms. Her father, always the realist, had declared that if a person's way of life conflicted with his religion, one or the other had to yield. And he moved to scrap the, to him, outdated religion. Barbara, too, is beginning to see that once given the true picture of the way her society operates, she cannot go on with her assumption that the Army can operate free from any hint of moral compromise. Were Barbara a true romantic, in the Shavian sense, she would have no difficulty in quieting her scruples. Her mother, her brother, and Lomax are romantics in this fashion, and so is the otherwise clear-headed Mrs. Baines. Barbara, however, like her father, insists upon a set of convictions that she can consistently live by. Those that have hitherto served her are now being put to the test. As her father shrewdly realizes, once she finds them wanting, she will be realist enough to drop them and look around for those that will prove more satisfying. At present, however, she is bewildered and uncertain.

## SIGNIFICANT THEMES

### Realism Vs. Romanticism

Mrs. Baines is a realist in her approach to the ruthless and practical munitions man. She is romantic, however, in naively accepting the hypocritical piety of Snobby Price. Barbara is realistic in her belief that true ease of conscience can never be merely a matter of money, but she is romantic in assuming that the Army will never accept tainted money.

## Crime And Punishment

Neither the humiliating meeting with Todger nor the offered pound provides the ideal answer to Bill's problem of conscience. Punishment, in the usual sense, would only leave him feeling free to repeat the offense.

## Evils Of Current Religion

The Army, by preaching love and resignation, encourages the poor to stop agitating for their rights and thus perpetuates injustice. Moreover, there is some suggestion that Mrs. Baines has had to do a certain amount of rationalizing to solicit funds from men like Bodger and Undershaft in the name of religion.

## Topic For Discussion

Is Bill Walker's persistent battle with conscience plausible? Or does the situation seem unusually contrived?

# MAJOR BARBARA

## TEXTUAL ANALYSIS

## ACT 2, SCENE 8; ACT 3, SCENE 1

### ACT II, SCENE 8

#### SUMMARY

As Bill laughs cynically at the deal, Barbara protests the acceptance of money from those whose products cause misery and degradation. Undershaft ironically argues that the Army can triumph over them by preaching sobriety and peace. Cusins with frenzied air prepares to join. Undershaft, Mrs. Baines, and Jenny in a march of thanksgiving, which he compares to a wild, pagan rite. Crushed, Barbara will not condemn Mrs. Baines, but hands over her own Army emblem to her father as victor. She adds that she may never again pray. When the marchers leave, Bill taunts her and makes her see the deceptions of Snobby and Rummy. But he leaves with an amiable farewell, still unconverted. Barbara gamely invites Shirley to have tea with her and tell her about his Secularist readings.

## Comment

This scene completes the first and most painful stage of Barbara's education, at the hands of the ruthlessly determined Undershaft. As it runs its course, her world seems to crash around her. The Army, in the person of the capable Mrs. Baines, welcomes a donation from its cynical arch enemies, for as Barbara points out, murder and drunkenness are hideous evils. And the relentless Undershaft boldly admits that he makes his money through senseless and sanguinary wars. Adolphus, curiously exhilarated by the spectacle, offers her no comforting support. And even the innocent and unquestionably devout Jenny Hill seems unconcernedly gratified over the extraordinary windfall. All around her the blows fall. "What price salvation?" Bill asks, his cockiness entirely restored, his need for spiritual solace no longer felt. And then Barbara must hear the meanly vindictive Rummy, who hitherto has mouthed pious sentiments in her presence, gloat over Snobby's sly purloining of Walker's pound. Her one friend in need is Shirley, who never did claim to have experienced any conversion.

Yet despite the shattering of her illusions and the destruction of her hopes, the granddaughter of the Earl is not entirely overwhelmed. She retains in this dark hour something of Lady Britomart's aristocratic manner and something of Undershaft's steely composure. Her presentation of her Army pin to her father is a magnificently scornful gesture, and she takes Bill's sneers of triumph with remarkably good grace. Then as the scene ends, her rueful but friendly invitation to tea extended to Peter Shirley has in it a flash of the old half-humorous managerial spirit.

Shaw has sometimes been accused of being a playwright much more concerned about ideas than about people. Some have claimed that there is a certain coldness in his plays. Certainly some of his heroes, such as the astute Julius Caesar in Caesar and Cleopatra or the wily Undershaft here may be interesting, even admirable in some ways, but they have about them a rather forbidding air of invulnerability. In this scene, Barbara's downfall is ordinarily a very moving experience for audiences. She is not only a spirited, likable personality, but a true idealist. And the heartbreak that she suffers seems painfully real.

Incidentally, her poignant cry, "My God: why hast thou forsaken me?" caused the play some trouble with the official censors of the time. There was some question as to whether or not there was something objectionable in having the heroine adopt the words of Christ spoken from the Cross. The difficulty was settled when the playwright pointed out that the passage could also be found in the Psalms.

A somewhat puzzling aspect of the scene is the desertion of Barbara by Adolphus. Technically, of course, the dramatist wants her to feel the full brunt of the disillusioning revelations forced by her father. And there will be less of a catastrophic effect, and, coincidentally, less chance for Barbara to prove her true mettle, if a strong and solicitous fiance is hovering near to soften blows and perk up morale.

As it stands however, the actual conduct of the classics professor is curious. He talks rather frenziedly of Dionysus, the god of vegetation and wine. There are various reasons, of course, for the association. Being linked with wine, the god's name would tie in with the talk of Bodger and his whiskey.

He was also considered a lover of peace, and Undershaft has been sardonically talking of the Army's efforts to discourage wars. Furthermore, some of the festivals in honor of the god were celebrated with rather wild and dissolute expressions of joy. And if Dionysus became on the one hand the patron of tragic art (and

Barbara's suffering has tragic overtones), he is also represented as surrounded by followers noted for madness or enthusiasm. Now the presumably sensitive and observant Cusins sees at once the enthusiastic cymbal-clanging delight of the Army leaders, the saturnine triumph of Undershaft, and the grief of Barbara. the combination seems to rouse in him an almost hysterical excitement. Although hardly in total sympathy with his future father-in-law, he is overcome with shocked amazement at the thoroughness of his carefully calculated campaign. He is not then necessarily insensitive when he leaves Barbara to join the march. He may rather be hypersensitive, roused to fever pitch by the observed interplay of diverse emotions. As he says, he is "possessed."

## CHARACTER ANALYSIS

### Andrew Undershaft

In this scene, several traits of the munitions czar are apparent. First of all, there is his intellectual power. He can make a quietly sardonic quip on the benefits of alcohol, or he can outline with terrifying clarity the dreadful havoc wrought during wars in which the weapons he sells are used, thus augmenting his already staggering profits. He thoroughly alarms Mrs. Baines, a kindly soul at heart, with his talk of innocent people slaughtered. The question is, why does he spell out so frightfully the destruction that his products unleash? Can there, further, be anything admirable in such a man?

For one thing, Undershaft, whose motto is "Unashamed," is being here brutally honest. He is shunning the polite subterfuges by which other philanthropists whitewash the questionable trades that produce the fortunes they distribute. He is not out to upset Mrs. Baines, of course. She is no real concern of his. But his plans for Barbara demand that there be essentially no deception as to what he is doing, where he stands, and what compromises the Army is prepared to make. Should the Army be in some doubt as to the exact source of the money he offers, then there might be left for Barbara some intellectual or moral loophole she could seize upon to keep her starry-eyed views. But he paints the worst possible picture, then hands the check to Mrs. Baines, who does not decline it but regards it as the work of "Infinite Goodness." This leaves Barbara no middle course. She must either compromise on her high, strict standards or give up the Army. And it is Undershaft's clear intention to force such a decision.

At the same time, there is something of the bold gambler in Undershaft. Having done his best or his worst to disillusion his daughter, he makes no move to help her or even communicate with her. He talks to Cusins about playing the trombone and maintains a generally jovial manner. Yet he is somewhat alarmed when Barbara advances toward him and pins her badge on his collar. And his quotation from Shylock in Shakespeare's *Merchant of Venice*, "My ducats and my daughter!" suggests that he may not be altogether certain whether his objective will be achieved. He has caused Barbara to break with the Army. But will she forgive him and become his "convert"? Much hangs in the balance, and a lesser individual might try frantically to mollify her. Not Undershaft. With iron control he goes off, leaving her to work out her own answers. Actually, he will educate her further in subsequent scenes. But for now only she herself can muster the courage needed for the uphill spiritual fight ahead.

Obviously there is little of the conventional loving father in Undershaft as he appears in this scene. He seems much closer to Cusins' "Mephistopheles." But Shaw evidently feels that he is destroying Barbara's false assumptions in the interests of presenting her with a higher, more valuable set of truths. Hence, though his methods may be harsh, he is still doing something commendable.

## Barbara Undershaft

Here, Barbara shows her true strength of character. In the first place, she is not one to evade bitter truths. she will not let pass her father's sardonic defense of the virtues of alcohol. And she will not attempt to explain away the Army's acceptance of the money, even though by so doing she might preserve something that has meant a great deal to her. She has considerable intellectual resilience, and does not flinch from the facts.

Naturally hurt by the actions of both her father and Cusins, she still never loses control of her emotions. She is no Rummy Mitchens to let loose with bitter invective. Her pinning of the emblem on her father's coat is a telling but restrained rebuke. And she can still be relatively courteous and pleasant to Bill and Shirley. Nor does she presume to judge or condemn Mrs. Baines even though she herself could never countenance the acceptance of such questionable contributions. Barbara's heart may be breaking, but she reacts to the dashing of her hopes like a lady. In fact, she arouses the grudging admiration even of the gloating Walker by conducting herself with that quiet courage that Hemingway has defined as "grace under pressure."

## Bill Walker

Like Barbara, Bill regards the accepting of the money as a matter of cynical betrayal. His conscience pound was rejected, but the lavish donations of unregenerate plutocrats are gratefully accepted. Barbara, of course, carefully points out that she did not take his pound, and it is obvious that she would not, had the decision been hers, have taken the checks either. But while Bill, by no means a liar like Price, will concede her consistency, he has further evidence of the Army's weaknesses in Snobby's stealing and Rummy's vindictive refusal to warn him of the theft. Barbara momentarily feels cheated. She had almost saved his soul, but now he is convinced that all is false. From the playwright's point of view, however, the education of Bill parallels to some extent that of Barbara. According to one critic, Joseph Frank, Bill has at least already learned two valuable lessons. His remorse makes it less probable that he will ever be guilty of the same type of offense again. And, in addition, he has begun to question the justice of society and is thus en route to true "salvation." Shaw would have the lower classes not humble and submissive, but proud and rebellious. For only if they show spirit, will they move to improve their lot. Bill already has this restless spirit ("'Major Barbara'-Shaw's 'Divine Comedy'," p. 67).

## Adolphus Cusins

As indicated above, Cusins reacts with intense nervous excitement to Undershaft's devastating tactics. Cusins, it is clear from the beginning, never believed in the Army the way that Barbara did. Still he found Undershaft's first declaration that the Army could be "bought" frankly incredible. As, however, he watches Undershaft in action and sees the havoc wrought, he reacts as one "possessed." Ordinarily, he would probably stand with Barbara. He reacted with fury when he thought that Undershaft was alleging that she could be bought. But at this point he seems to feel curiously helpless as though all were in the grip of irresistible force. So he goes off with wild, almost mad elation to join in the Army's march f triumph celebrating its rescue by Bodger and Undershaft.

## Peter Shirley

Shirley has served several purposes in the drama. He has been the starving discharged worker, proving how callous and wasteful can be some operations under capitalism. Secondly, he has been mean and cantankerous enough to add further proof that destitution does not encourage nobility. Thirdly, his obvious sense of humiliation has demonstrated one more evil of poverty.

He has also, however, been identified clearly throughout as a Secularist. And now Barbara, needing someone to prevent her feeling too sorry for herself, invites him to join her for tea. She will then listen to his talk of Paine and Bradlaugh. Thomas Paine was an eighteenth-century writer on political and other subjects. His *The Rights of Man* helped to stimulate much early revolutionary feeling and his *The Age of Reason* was a violent, extreme attack on traditional Christianity. As for Charles Bradlaugh, he was a famous atheistic lecturer of Shaw's own time. He and Shaw had written for a magazine started by the freethinking Mrs. Annie Besant. Shirley's views are never going to be explored further in the play. And it is not clear whether Barbara is really interested in them as a possible substitute for her lost faith or whether she merely wants to put him at ease and let him talk on his favorite subjects. In any event the proud and stubborn Shirley has never been an Army convert, and, in general, as was pointed out in the section on Bill Walker, Shaw prefers those who tend to think in revolutionary rather than submissive terms. Undershaft sharply corrected Shirley when he talked of being proud of being poor. That, to Shaw, would be unavailing cant. But a Shirley proud enough to question the system is something else. A man like that may work for necessary progress.

## SIGNIFICANT THEMES

### Salvation

The salvation that can be bought, according to Barbara and later the ironic Bill, cannot be a true salvation. Barbara probably thought of herself as "saved" when she was with the Army. To Shaw, however, her true salvation begins when she sheds her illusions and starts on the road to a higher truth.

### Evils Of Capitalism

Undershaft spells out with awesome exactitude the evils resulting from such lucrative industries as those of liquor and armaments. Shaw, a teetotaler, usually treats drinking as an unmitigated curse.

### Evils Of Current Religion

The Army can only survive by accepting the money of the wealthy, regardless of how it was originally made. It can thus be forced into the position of preaching peace with armaments funds and inveighing against drunkenness with contributions provided by distillers. Furthermore, the ineffectual spiritual side of the Army is again stressed by the revelation of Snobby's theft and Rummy's spite. Finally, the rather startling ability of Mrs. Baines to see in the action of the "infernal" Undershaft the blessings of "Infinite Goodness" suggests that religious individuals are capable of some rather sweeping rationalizations.

## TOPICS FOR DISCUSSION

Is Barbara's decisive renouncing of the Army a convincing move? Or does Shaw, to bring this about, have to picture her as either incredibly naive or unusually fanatical? Also, are the actions of Cusins made plausible, as having quickly dismissed Barbara's claim that he breaks her heart, he talks of being "possessed," thanks to "Dionysus Undershaft"?

## ACT III, SCENE 1

### SUMMARY

The next afternoon, back in the Wilton Crescent library, Lomax tries clumsily to cheer up Barbara, no longer in uniform. Adolphus enters, somewhat pale and shaky. After the Army's victory meeting, Undershaft, a non-drinker, had plied him with wine. He and Barbara agree that despite family ties Undershaft has yet to win over their souls. Later conferring alone with his wife, Undershaft agrees to provide income for the girls, but again firmly refuses to leave the business to Stephen, whom he finds singularly unimpressive. He admits, however, that he has yet found no promising foundlings, for the intelligent ones are now educated by charitable foundations to become conventionally second-rate. Joining them, Stephen angers his mother and delights Undershaft by turning down the cannon works in advance. He also loftily rejects the arts, philosophy, the armed services, the law, the church, and the stage. He does, however, clearly know, he claims, how to tell right from wrong. So his amused and skeptical father suggests a career in politics or journalism, but warns the smugly incredulous youth that such powerful industrialists as he actually control both government and press.

## Comment

These initial incidents in Act III give audiences a chance to learn, first of all, how the various characters have been affected by the rather explosive developments that occurred at the Army shelter. Barbara, who now appears in the fashionable attire of a young upper-class woman, seems weary and discouraged. Lomax, essentially good-hearted, is as voluble and foolish as ever, Sarah as languid, and Lady Britomart as fussily authoritarian. There has, in fact, been little change in Wilton Crescent proper. The arrival of Adolphus, with an obvious hangover, does stir up some excitement, since apparently he was never known as a drinking man. But, essentially, his coming is used to point up four facts.

First of all, it brings out anew the cool-hearted efficiency of Undershaft. Shaw's men of destiny, like their creator, are not likely to take refuge in alcohol. Undershaft provided plenty of wine for Cusins but drank none himself. Secondly, Cusins brings news of the meeting, which was unusually successful, resulting in over a hundred conversions. Just in case Barbara or the audience might suspect that there was some later change of heart about accepting the Bodger and Undershaft assistance, this settles decisively that matter. Furthermore, Cusins' reference to the wild emotionalism at the meeting would be in line with Shaw's critical attitude toward this type of religious experience.

Thirdly, the scene makes it clear how matters stand between Cusins and Barbara. Despite his desertion of the previous day and his present tardy arrival, she does not seem angry. She has done some thinking, nevertheless, and is now fairly sure that his "conversion" to the Army, as her family knew all along, was mainly to be at her side. She is relieved, however, to learn that he has not as yet, wine or no wine, wholly surrendered to the persuasive Undershaft. Finally, the arrival of Cusins indicates how the young people feel at this moment about Barbara's father. Cusins assures Barbara that he is convinced of Undershaft's affection for her. But Barbara still talks of "larger loves" and "diviner dreams" as being more important than mere family relationships. Cusins agrees that Undershaft must win him, too, on "holier ground." So the two are not hostile, but not by any means totally converted yet to what the critic Joseph Frank has called "Undershaftianity." This lays the groundwork for the crucial efforts of the millionaire to overcome all their objections when they go to visit his cannon works.

As for the subsequent encounter between Undershaft and his wife, and their disconcerting interview with the obdurate Stephen, there is first evident a strong element of standard domestic comedy. Undershaft irks his stiffly dignified wife by calling her "Biddy," not "Britomart." And she, in turn, throws him somewhat off-balance by telling him his tie is crooked. And even had Shaw no serious criticism in mind at all, the maddeningly superior airs of the unambitious, untalented, unimaginative Stephen would be quite funny. And the bafflement of both parents in trying to provide a glittering future for so uncooperative a scion would amuse many with only the mildest interest in the dramatist's social theories.

Yet the **episodes** do have some Shavian views to advance. For one thing, there is Shaw's disgust with contemporary education. Stephen is identified as a product of the best British schools. Yet Stephen has developed no capabilities and had never entertained any suggestion that there might be need for change or progress. He thinks of himself as an expert moralist, but really knows nothing about the complexities of the human situation. In addition, he has only the most guileless textbook notions about government. Britain to him, apparently, is ruled exclusively by independent gentlemen like himself, of irreproachable manners and morals. Worst of all, he has an almost completely closed mind. Having accepted without question all the extremely conservative and orthodox ideas taught him, he has no urge to ask any questions or pay heed to any new opinions. To Shaw, in other words, nothing in England's conventional education system at that time would encourage its graduates to pitch in and work for progress. Shaw himself, of course, had only a limited exposure to formal schooling. To complete the criticism, he has Undershaft snort at the efforts of such charitable institutions as the Barnado homes for poor children to educate likely lads. They, too, are corrupted by a training that crams them with shopworn ideas and induces them to conform submissively to whatever is the prevailing taste. Should he leave his munitions business either to his son or to a foundling who had been exposed to such a stultifying program, eventually some abler individual, possibly from Italy or Germany, would forge ahead by being much more enterprising and inventive. Shaw often, incidentally, held up foreigners as more progressive than the English, and during his last years, his praise of Russia's communistic system antagonized many.

This section also expresses Shaw's impatience with other aspects of contemporary British life. Three areas of attack may be singled out: government, journalism, and moral criticism. First of all, he objects to Stephen's idealistic view that the British government is run impartially and independently by cultivated men of sterling integrity. Instead, he sharply declares, great capitalists like Undershaft, through their newspapers and other interests, are the true masters of government. The rest are merely figureheads. His statement is quite extreme, and it is debatable just how literally Shaw means his view to be accepted. But it is consistent with the play's whole line of thinking about the importance of money and power. And, certainly, it is a useful corrective to Stephen's vastly oversimplified conception of how great modern states are run.

As for journalism, Shaw's sniping is at first surprising, since he himself as music and drama critic had for some years been a member of the profession. Yet he criticizes again and again all who help to bolster the present imperfect system by fostering "romantic" or nonrealistic conceptions of its true nature. Stephen's notion of the impeccable character of British political leaders is the sort of thing either credulous or merely partisan writers might publish, thus discouraging again any thought that improvements were needed. Such journalists are therefore to be repudiated. It may be worth mentioning that Shaw is also rather hard on newspapermen in his next play after *Major Barbara*, called *The Doctor's Dilemma*.

Finally, he takes issue with those who, like Stephen or even naive Jenny Hill, think that all moral questions can be easily resolved. It must be remembered that Shaw himself rejects some aspects of traditional Christianity and accepts others. And he tends to suggest at times that values are relative, that what may be right for one may be wrong for another. He has Undershaft, for instance, earlier in the play, say that his true faith is that of the armorer, but this may not be a true faith for everyone. And Barbara, even while she is certain that she would never accept the Undershaft and Bodger checks, will not tell Mrs. Baines that she was "wrong." In any event, Shaw has no patience with those who think that matters of morality, any more than those of economics, politics, philosophy, or religion, were once and for all settled long ago. He is always in favor of keeping the discussion going.

## CHARACTER ANALYSIS

### Andrew Undershaft

As in his first appearance, Undershaft is again the genial older gentleman amiably settling family matters and a little flustered when his wife points out that his tie is askew. Nevertheless, he can still be the ruthless magnate when the occasion demands. He lets his wife know in no uncertain manner that he has no intention whatsoever of being swayed in his decision to leave the business to someone other than his unimpressive son. And he brusquely declares to the frankly unbelieving Stephen that whatever the young man may believe, he, Undershaft, is the power behind his country's government. It is also worth noting that he indicates that he can easily make a place for Stephen in any line of endeavor that his son happens to fancy. This, again, suggests his own unlimited potential. The scene also, however, suggests that Undershaft admires Barbara and would like her to marry a competent foundling and thus carry on the Undershaft tradition. Barbara, however, is engaged to Cusins, and that apparent difficulty will have to be cleared up.

### Lady Britomart Undershaft

As in earlier scenes the Earl's daughter is determined to ward off any affectionate overtures on the part of her husband and to force him in some way to favor Stephen's interests. Again, however, she is frustrated. Andrew will not hear of her plan, and Stephen himself first refuses summarily to go into any business and then urges his mother rather haughtily not to interfere further. But as a comic character Lady Britomart has two good moments. One occurs when she insists that the slangy Lomax grow up and start taking his "formulas" of wisdom from the *London Times.* She admits that the ideas may not always be right, but they will be tolerably well expressed. This is an amusing speech, which, of course, ironically glances at Shaw's dislike for all "formula" thinking. The other opportunity to shine is her sudden breaking up of Undershaft's rather pompous declaration with the remark that his tie is crooked. This is a nice feminine tactic, worthy of, say, Ann in *Man and Superman,* (or even Mrs. Day, in the modern American comedy, *Life With Father*).

## Barbara Undershaft

Despite the blows of yesterday, Barbara has retained her composure and matter-of-fact good sense. When the well-meaning Cholly becomes a nuisance, she sends him over amiably to lavish affection upon Sarah, to the latter's mild annoyance. She seems to bear no grudge against Cusins but inquires solicitously as to his state of mind. She has left off her uniform and so has apparently given up the Army, but perhaps out of womanly curiosity still wants to hear about the meeting. Above all, she still wants something more than ordinary domestic satisfactions. Her concern remains with "larger loves and diviner dreams." And it is quite clear that neither a father's affection nor even a husband's tenderness is going to be enough for her. These are "fireside" delights and pleasant to experience. But Barbara, like her father, has something about her of the "confirmed mystic." This, curiously, will be evident again in an upcoming scene when she declares rather surprisingly, for an engaged girl, that she would rather lose Adolphus than be deprived of the chance to convert Walker. But it must be remembered that Barbara is a

Shavian heroine, that is, a character regarded favorably by her creator. And Shaw never approves of those who put their own personal satisfactions above life's demand for selfless service to further the progress of humanity.

## Adolphus Cusins

Much calmer than in the previous scene, Dolly lets it be known that whereas he still finds Undershaft impressive, he has not yet accepted all of the older man's views. During or after a convivial evening, he still demands that Barbara's father win him on "holier ground" even though they are already united in their mutual fondness for the girl. In so voicing his hesitation, Cusins, of course, says precisely what Barbara hopes to hear. For she herself is by no means wholly satisfied with her father's position and would probably experience again the heartbreak known yesterday were she to feel once more that the two men had joined forces completely.

## Stephen Undershaft

Undershaft's son is here made to provide the best possible argument against the ordinary system by which sons inherit directly from their fathers. And it will be recalled that Shaw had encountered in the writings of Auguste Comte the idea that great enterprises were some sort of sacred public trust to be handed down only to those well fitted to promote future progress. Undershaft, on his part, does not deny that the very momentum he has established would enable Stephen to get along for a time with the services of able managers. But Stephen essentially has nothing new to contribute, and hence eventually the industrial empire would collapse.

Stephen's almost complete lack of interest in any of the leading fields of human activity is a matter almost of caricature. Shaw uses his portrayal here, however, for three purposes. First of all, the very succession of work areas suggested and declined is amusing. It has in it the type of rhythmic repetition that builds to a **climax** and almost always gets laughs. Secondly, as indicated above, it implies a harshly critical attitude toward the moribund educational system that turned out this incompetent young gentleman. Finally, the series of denials prepares for Stephen's claim to be expert in distinguishing right from wrong, thus giving Undershaft, speaking for Shaw, the chance to attack devastatingly all such foolish pretentions.

### Charles Lomax

As before, the object of Lady Britomart's withering rebukes, Lomax makes more vapid attempts to be helpful, only to be generally snubbed. Lady Britomart urges him to start learning "formulas" from such highly respectable publications as *The Spectator*, a magazine held in some esteem, and the unassailable *Times,* London's most famous newspaper. Lomax may or may not take her advice, but he is momentarily subdued by her managerial manner, just as he merely obeyed the strong-minded Barbara when she sent him over to "spoon" with Sarah.

## SIGNIFICANT THEMES

### Wealth And Power

Undershaft makes it clear that because of his position as a highly successful capitalist, he can control the government and the press.

### Failure Of Conventional Education

Stephen has neither the talent nor the training to contribute anything to human progress, and he has almost no receptivity to new ideas. Furthermore, Undershaft has found that the poor boys, helped through scholarship grants, also lose most of their initiative and incentive to think creatively by the time they have been thoroughly trained.

### Religious Dedication

Barbara and Cusins will never be satisfied with mere "fireside" satisfactions. They have need of greater objects to pursue. In this they resemble Undershaft and differ from others in the group.

### Realism Vs. Romanticism

Stephen is a romantic in his concept of the British government. He should get along well with equally nonrealistic journalists.

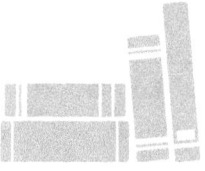

# MAJOR BARBARA

## TEXTUAL ANALYSIS

## ACT 3, SCENES 2 AND 3

### ACT III, SCENE 2

#### SUMMARY

The group prepares to view the Undershaft works, but Cusins is the only man who will ride with Undershaft in the latter's unpainted, experimental car. The munitions maker surprises them with the news that his workers live in a clean, pleasant country town. He never has to give harsh orders, but his men, all snobs, are strict with those under supervision, thus increasing his profits. Barbara still bitterly regrets having had Walker's soul snatched from her, but her father cheers her with the idea that she did have a good effect. Having arrived in Undershaft's idyllic Perivale St. Andrews, Sarah and Stephen become enthusiastic, but Barbara and Cusins are still skeptical. Stephen does question the pampering of the workers, but Undershaft says organizing civilization decreases fears and difficulties. Lomax causes some excitement by lighting a cigarette near explosives, and Lady Britomart eyes the attractive homes acquisitively. The foundling question arises again, and Cusins stuns them by claiming that he technically qualifies because of a legal flaw in his parents' marriage. Undershaft is interested, and Cusins forces him to offer a fantastically high salary. The moral question remains.

## Comment

In this set of brief incidents several things are accomplished. As the family leaves, for instance, Cusins is contrasted with Lomax. Lomax, stolidly conventional, will not ride in the odd-looking experimental automobile driven by the unintimidated Undershaft. Cusins, however, will take the risk of shocking the neighbors. At this point, it is also made clear that Barbara is still disturbed by what happened at the shelter. Undershaft astutely consoles her by assuring her that she may well have had a stronger influence upon Walker than she suspects. She feels better, but Cusins suspects some clever ambiguity. It must be understood that salvation may mean something quite different to Undershaft than it does to Barbara. If Undershaft here is following the general Shavian line, he probably means that she has stirred up Bill's thinking enough to render it less likely that he will ever be one of the weak, submissive types who do nothing to secure their rights. Barbara, however, probably still has a quite different idea, although actually her beliefs are none too clear following her break with the Army.

This section of Act III is also concerned with clearing up the misconception that all have about Undershaft's munitions town. Instead of a dark, smoke-ridden inferno, it is a bright and attractive rural village with comfortable dwellings and white churches. Sarah and Stephen are enchanted with the nursing home and the library, the school and the fine, inexpensive restaurant. And Lady Britomart cannot conceal delighted amazement at the good furniture and splendid gardens. Suddenly she wanted to own and run the whole town.

This idealized representation of Perivale St. Andrews, a mythical town, of course, serves several dramatic purposes. In the first place, it would probably prove as astonishing to Shaw's audience as it would to the young Undershafts. In the first decade of the twentieth century there may have been considerable talk about improving the lot of the working class, but the conditions described in the play would be very rare indeed. Acting partly out of intelligent self-interest and partly from some "mystic" conviction of being used by some higher power, Undershaft has set up a type of community that many would describe as "utopian."

In working out his theories in the play, Shaw has, to be sure, tended to deal in extreme cases. Snobby and Rummy are surely the least lovable examples of how poverty can warp the spirit. Bodger and Undershaft are carefully chosen as representing the industries most likely to be criticized on moral grounds. And so, the munitions town, standing for the good uses to which dubious profits can be put, will be more shining and more strikingly geared for over-all comfort than any other conceivable spot. Unlike West Ham, which is relatively authentic, this is a dream town. And audiences could undoubtedly share the pleased astonishment of Stephen, Sarah, and Lady Britomart.

Intellectually, of course, it symbolizes the new idea that even the most conservative gentry may someday be brought to recognize and appreciate. Hitherto Sarah has been listless and bored, Stephen obdurately unresponsive, and Lady Britomart interested solely in her son's heritage. Having been moved physically out of Wilton Crescent into a totally new world of industry and progress, even they show signs of life. All reveal an enthusiasm never witnessed up to now except in Barbara and Cusins.

At the same time, the more limited minds are impressed almost exclusively by the material and by the superficial aspects. This attitude is not entirely to be condemned. For Undershaft has stressed all along that without good material surroundings, man cannot achieve his highest level of living. Yet a noticeable contrast is drawn between the immediately convinced group and the warier Barbara and Ctsins. The outside of Perivale St. Andrews they, too, find admirable. But what of its inner life, of its soul? These two, represented as deeper than the rest, must know more before they give unqualified approval.

As for the contention by Cusins that he is a "foundling" because of a legal quibble, this is a shamelessly contrived way of settling a rather silly plot question, even though the idea of "new blood" in the firm may well have been serious. Shaw is against stagnation in all areas! As the problem is worked out, it inevitably recalls some of the wilder **denouements** of Gilbert and Sullivan operettas. We remember, for instance, the apprentice outlaw in *The Pirates of Penzance* and the impossibility switched infants in *H.M.S. Pinafore*. And it is by no means impossible that Shaw is poking some fun, as indeed Gilbert and Sullivan were, at some of the implausible devices of romantic fiction.

At the same time he has Cusins blandly use the word "subterfuge." And the move by Adolphus is used to point up the streak of adventurous daring, if not out-and-out opportunism, that really does create a bond between the present Andrew Undershaft, and the future one, Adolphus being required to adopt his patron's name if the deal is concluded. This almost reckless effrontery is again brought out when Cusins boldly demands much more of a salary than Undershaft ever intended a prospective heir to seek. There is bravado here, but this is the sort of "madness" that Shaw and, naturally, Undershaft admire.

There is one almost exclusively humorous incident in which Lomax, against all prudent warnings, refuses to recognize the danger of lighting a match near a shed with explosives. His stupidity, reminiscent of Stephen's on other occasions, is amusing in itself, and it, of course, points up once more the colossal assurance and crass ignorance of the upper classes. But, in addition, it brings in the dramatic element of danger with which Shaw would balance his vision of rustic peace and plenty. The good life represented here is secured only through "blood and fire." Undershaft gloats over war in remote Manchuria. He does not care in the least which side wins so long as he sells more armaments. This prosperity, like the continuance of the Army's work at the shelter, can be maintained only through the industry's marketing of lethal products. Undershaft would not let Mrs. Baines forget this. Shaw keeps the same disturbing idea before Barbara, Cusins, and his audience.

## CHARACTER ANALYSIS

### Barbara Undershaft

Although she has been quiet and agreeable enough since the act began, Barbara is shown to be still brooding over her failure to convert Bill, and she rather bitterly holds her father responsible. Yet let him murmur something vaguely comforting about her influence, and her joy is restored. At times Barbara's nature seems curiously simple and childlike, as will be suggested when she tugs at her mother's skirts as the play ends.

It is evident once more in this section that Barbara misses the exaltation she felt while working with the Army and feels a sense of loss. Her father explains that she has been learning something new, and that the experience is sometimes painful. Upon arriving at the works, she remains skeptical. Where is the spiritual element in all this material comfort? And as Cusins excitedly drives his hard bargain with Undershaft, she wonders if Dolly is now selling his soul in a manner recalling the Army's surrender of the previous day. She even half suggests that she may give up Cusins if he is really giving up his principles for lucre. Barbara still wants a great work to do on behalf of a noble cause. She has not yet found the answer.

## Adolphus Cusins

Having proved that he is not so rigidly conventional as Lomax by volunteering to ride with Undershaft in the latter's unpainted experimental car, Cusins asserts his independence further at the foundry. His object there is to see whatever he is not supposed to see. Unlike Sarah and Stephen, for instance, he is not entirely convinced. He has not been able to discover the flaw, and there are churches clearly in evidence. But he instinctively feels that here amid all this apparent perfection there is something hellish, infernal. And, upon hearing Undershaft cheerfully announce that his very efficient "aerial battleship" has killed three hundred soldiers in far-distant Manchuria, Cusins is sickened.

Yet he seems determined to get control of the business. Excitedly he makes his surprising announcement that he can qualify as a "foundling," admitting to Barbara that he has been studying the whole question since the previous day. He has ready, if dubious, answers for all Undershaft's objections, and puts up an astonishing battle for the highest possible salary. All in all, his motivation appears complex. Having been observing Undershaft carefully since they met, he knows that the older man, being strong and ruthless himself, will probably have respect only for someone equally relentless and unyielding. Since a professor of Greek, who for love of a girl has banged a drum for the Salvation Army, will not automatically be regarded as a shrewd, hard-driving executive type, so Cusins, to some extent, is putting on a demonstration to impress Undershaft. Undeniably, too, for all his claims of being romantic, Cusins is personally ambitious. His aspirations are partially connected with his love for Barbara. He became quite angry when Undershaft questioned his ability to support her, and he admits that he feared being considered an "adventurer" out to ensnare a rich wife. Yet his obvious dismay over the reported war casualties and certain other references as to the approval of his conscience suggest that he may have some even higher motive in attempting to succeed Undershaft.

## Andrew Undershaft

Although from the first, he has regarded Cusins with some interest, Undershaft seems somewhat unprepared for the young man's strenuous efforts to be named munitions heir apparent. Yet he is used to coolly handling the unexpected and thoughtfully considers the possibilities. As he yields considerably on the salary question, the suspicion arises that it amuses him to humor the bold, and obviously inexperienced young "shark." He can always appreciate a good bluff, and besides, Barbara and whoever Barbara marries are to figure in his long-range plans. So clearly he allows himself to be talked out of more money in a way he would doubtless never permit any business rival to attempt. The triumphant Cusins gloats youthfully over his victory. But Undershaft is still as much in command as when he takes the dangerous matches from the imprudent Lomax, all the while gravely listening to his foolish talk about not losing courage when surrounded by high explosives.

In this scene, Undershaft reveals one further Machiavellian trait. One of the recognizable characteristics of this type of individual was a skill in selecting scapegoats. No matter what villainies these unprincipled opportunists devised, they saw to it that someone else was set up to take the blame. Undershaft has a Jewish partner, Lazarus, who apparently has very little actual part in running the business. Undershaft pictures him rather as gentle, "romantic," interested in concerts and plays. But apparently because of general anti-Semitic prejudice, Lazarus is held responsible for all of Undershaft's greed and avarice. And Undershaft predicts that he will be condemned in the future for that of Cusins. In this passage, Shaw gives us some further understanding of the sharp, sometimes devious Undershaft. Also, however, he eyes critically those who would unthinkingly blame all economic ills upon the Jews and thus never call to an accounting the real culprits.

## SIGNIFICANT THEMES

### Benefits Of Economic Security

At first glance Undershaft's pampering of his workers would not seem to have made them more content. As he describes conditions in his plant, the workers at each level snub and harshly keep in line all on the levels beneath them. And, curiously, Shirley, who has been given a job and a fine house, is raising bitter objections. Undershaft's claim is that this type of iron rule exercised by his subordinates over other subordinates benefits him in two ways. For one thing, it leaves him free to be kindly and benevolent. For another, it increases efficiency and adds to his profits. At the same time, he notes that life there has been so organized that there is no real care and anxiety save that connected with handling explosives. The point is that Shaw hates poverty because it not only causes sickness and other physical miseries but also causes men to be docile, undemanding slaves. To Shaw the spirit of grumbling and rebellion holds promise of some efforts to improve conditions further. Here the people are not sick, dirty, ignorant, or feeble. And they are not hopelessly submissive either.

## Salvation

Both Barbara and Cousins remain skeptical, even having seen the impressive beauties of Perivale St. Andrews. From Shaw's point of view, Undershaft has obviously done more than the Army to make life better for humbler men. But something still seems missing, something that will add the "heaven," that Barbara and her fiance still find missing in this "perfect triumph of modern industry."

## ACT III, SCENE 3

### SUMMARY

> Still suffering from moral scruples, Cusins is urged by Lady Britomart to sell the guns only to good people. Undershaft, however, insists that he keep the Armorer's faith of selling impartially to all who will pay. Cusins says he will do as he pleases, but Undershaft says that he is driven by a mysterious "will." In return Cusins calls him the tool of rascals, to which Undershaft replies that when the virtuous fight harder, he will sell to them too. Barbara regrets her lost faith, but her father declares that faulty old creeds like faulty machines

must be summarily scrapped. He warns her further not to underrate his town's cleanliness and prosperity. After all, he saved even her soul by keeping her well housed and fed. Only when the pressures of want are removed can the spirit soar. Poverty to him is the worst of crimes, destroying society far more completely than do murders and robberies. He could save Walker for her by giving him a good job. He himself, once a poor man, resolved to be rich at any price and can now be generous and kind. Scorning Cusins' talk of love and pity, and other protests offered by the rest, he states that to accomplish good one must wield power. Will Cusins dare war against war? Left alone with Barbara, Cusins tells her that he has decided to accept Undershaft's offer. She, for her part, has learned that rejecting Bodger and Undershaft is turning away from life. She will no longer bribe souls with bread and treacle. She will do God's work among her father's well-fed, snobbish workers. The Major has returned to the colors!

## Comment

This final scene, except for occasional half-humorous interruptions by the minor figures, is almost a presentation of certain serious Shavian theories. Essentially there are two main elements. One is summed up in the statement that poverty is the worst of evils, more dangerous and destructive than any of the usually dreaded crimes. Poverty leaves masses of people weak, sick, dirty, and miserable. Even in the physical sense, this is bad for the rest of society. Diseases can spread. Morally it is even worse, for to protect themselves against the legitimate anger of the wretched, those in power must build up police forces that inflict horrible penalties on those with spirit enough to rise up. And when not hypocritically salving their consciences with charity donations, they encourage the spread of a religion that preaches humility and resignation to those who should be demanding their fair share.

The second element involves the soaring of the spirit, about which Barbara and probably Adolphus feel great concern. The argument here is that men must first feel relatively free from the millstones of want before they can fulfill their spiritual destinies. Once their bodies are fed, the hunger of their souls will be most apparent. Then they will not have to be "bribed" with bread, such bribes being in the long run no more availing than they were with Snobby and Rummy. Instead, presumably, Barbara's new converts will take on some of the high-minded sense of personal dedication noticeable in Barbara herself. It is not altogether clear what specifically her message will be. She evidently does not admire overindulgence in drink, although Perivale St. Andrews does not seem given to drunken orgies. Certainly she is against brutality of all sorts, as evidenced in the Jenny Hill incident, and might try to discourage whatever there is of meanness or cruelty. Certainly, she will work as she did with Bill Walker to rouse consciences. In general, apparently, she will try to make her people act less selfishly, more generously in such a way as to better conditions for other men. And, meanwhile, presumably Cusins will try to give those still sorely oppressed the power to move up to the level of already well-fed Undershaft workers, thus becoming eligible for more of Barbara's ministrations. Above all, there must be no "bribe of heaven." All must do "God's work," that is, whatever is demanded from them to raise the general level of living, for the satisfaction of doing what is good, and not through expectation of a blissful eternity. Both Undershaft and Barbara feel that they are in the grip of some great power, probably Shaw's "life force," and are satisfied to know that they are cooperating with some vast benevolent plan. Barbara's "return to the colors" leaves some issues in doubt. Will she again be literally a Major in the

Salvation Army? If so, will she modify considerably the Army's teaching? Shaw does not specify.

Much of the scene is concerned with the decision of Cusins and with Barbara's objections. Her "conversion" is handled very briefly. She is given a new sense of exaltation and a new field of ministry, but much is left unexplained. Indeed there has been quite some critical objection to this on the grounds that her change of attitude is implausible. But Shaw has as his main concern here the idea that noble aspirations can be best developed in an environment of economic security. Having once made this point, he is content to end the discussion.

The other question of Cusins and the munitions works is also never wholly clarified. There is much talk of loving the common people and furnishing them with the power to secure justice. But how this is to be done is never indicated. Is Dolly going to provide free weapons for revolutionists? Or is he going to withhold them from governments unless they act more equitably? Certainly both he and Undershaft have indicated that nothing much can be accomplished merely by voting. Again there is the suggestion of the good cause to be advanced. Cusins is going to use the great armaments business in some way to make war on war. But the ways and means are left to the imagination. Shaw is content to stress first the need for power if any good is to be affected, and second, the need for courage and determination on the part of men of vision.

## CHARACTER ANALYSIS

### Andrew Undershaft

Here the poor boy who became a multimillionaire industrialist sums up his case. Poverty is the worst of evils and by unremitting effort he has saved himself, his family, and his workers from this most dreadful of blights. He has not been worried about traditional codes. If he had to kill to get ahead, he would. In his scale of values, nothing is worse than being poor. And he has consistently lived up to his own principles. He does not want love-that would imply weakness-merely, heed and respect. And he is most grateful to whoever opposes him so effectively that he must always be on the alert. No stagnation for Andrew! He admits that his control of things is not complete. He may give orders to newspapers and governments, but he in turn is being used by a power of which he is a part. And he clearly derives a sort of religious satisfaction from this sense of cooperating with forces that are beyond him. An able, energetic, forceful man, clearheaded and resourceful, he is also the "confirmed mystic," conscious of transforming society while he heaps up his profits. Some critics have claimed that he makes Shaw the arch apologist for capitalism, but others feel that he sees the Undershaft achievement as a transition stage between capitalism and socialism with Undershaft helping effect a gradual change by improving one small segment of society which in turn will improve others. Whichever is true. Shaw has clearly held many of his views and practices up to admiration.

## Barbara Undershaft

Urged to scrap her old ideas for more workable new ones, Barbara still hesitates, appalled at the dreadful havoc munitions can cause. Yet she is glad that Cusins makes an independent decision to accept the business. A true Undershaft, she admires boldness and daring. At the same time, her father's talk and actions have forced her to acknowledge that Bodger and Undershaft, that is, wealth from industry, influence all phases of English civilization. To turn one's back on them is therefore to reject life altogether. Eager to do her share, she finally decides she can serve best among the well-fed workers of her father's and her future husband's munitions works. There she will again draw people to highest and holiest things, teaching them to join her in doing God's work for its own sake. Her speech about getting rid of the "bribe for bread" and the "bribe of heaven" is usually very effective dramatically. But it is not altogether clear. Some have wondered whether or not, for instance, the pampered workers here are not, to some extent, bribed with bread? In addition, her high talk of making God grateful to her and of forgiving him "as becomes a woman of my rank," has seemed to many rather confusing. All that can be urged is that Shaw tends to equate God with that "life force" that is forever impelling human creatures, and especially the more enlightened, to help raise the level of the race. In this sense the life-force deity, able to achieve its ends only through such superior individuals, might be grateful, if it had really any heart to show any such feeling. The terms, however, are to most audiences somewhat obscure. What they see is a charming and vivacious girl, radiant once more, about to give with joy some sort of unselfish, vaguely religious service on behalf of humanity. She is also going to marry a bright young man with a great future and work happily along with him in a bright, cheerful town. Even audiences, it is claimed, who cannot or will not follow the serious arguments, are pleased to have this generally satisfactory "romantic" ending.

### Adolphus Cusins

No longer worried about the moral implications of making munitions, Dolly, who will soon assume the name of his benefactor, Andrew Undershaft, is prepared to use whatever power he acquires to help the common people, whom he loves. Incidentally, he makes his decision without consulting Barbara.

Shaw has no patience with those who place such personal matters as their love affairs above their serious work in life. Cusins is not particularly definite as to how he proposes to help the ordinary folk protect themselves against lying and oppressive intellectuals. He does say that he once gave a favorite student, headed for the wars, a revolver rather than a copy of Plato. But much remains unanswered. He says he is selling his soul for reality and power and that he means to use both for good ends. Meanwhile he will marry Barbara, and, according to Undershaft, come in to start learning the business at six the next morning. What else he will learn from the more harshly practical Undershaft is anybody's guess.

## SIGNIFICANT THEMES

### Evils Of Poverty

In a long, impassioned speech, Undershaft points out how poverty proves injurious to all levels of society. To him the seven deadly sins are not those of pride, greed, and lust, but of food, clothing, and whatever else burden the poor so that their spirits can never soar. To him a man's first obligation is not to be poor.

### Importance Of Wealth And Power

Cusins accepts the munitions post because he has been made to realize that he cannot really accomplish any good in the world unless he has money and influence. Barbara, aware of the pervasive effects of the industrialists' wealth, decides that facing life means accepting Bodger and Undershaft. Her father has insisted that she herself was saved only through his financial support.

## Love Relationships As Secondary

Undershaft is not much concerned about whether or not he is loved. Cusins decides that he will take the business regardless of what Barbara will say. She has already indicated that the saving of souls means more to her than Cusins.

## Salvation

To Shaw the whole matter of salvation means essentially cooperating with the life force and raising the level of mankind. Cusins will try to use his power to get the common people more chance to rise. Barbara will try to elevate the thinking of those already well fed. Good work will be their salvation and will achieve the salvation of others.

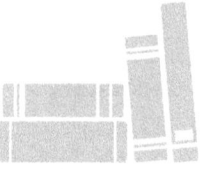

# MAJOR BARBARA

## ANALYSES OF MAJOR CHARACTERS

### ANDREW UNDERSHAFT

This alert, resourceful, determined munitions manufacturer is in many ways a typical Shavian hero. Essentially, Shaw seems to admire powerful men of superior intellect, who, having worked out for themselves a satisfying philosophy of life, decide what they want and go after it.

Genial and easy-going in manner, Undershaft almost never lets his guard down. He is generally in control of himself first, and of others insofar as they figure in his carefully laid plans. He is not likely to be swayed by emotions into losing sight of any vital objective. He may feel some affection for his wife, but he will not yield an inch on the matter of the foundling tradition. And he is never going to go out and drink with Adolphus, although he will play the generous host.

Above all, he is strictly honest with himself and with most other people, except possibly while engaged in some specific little Machiavellian scheme. He is not one, for instance, to deny his ruthless opportunism in business. His motto is "Unashamed," and he has no apologies to make for his concentration upon heaping up profits from the sale of weapons and explosives.

He is hardly a warm, likable type in the usual sense. Yet to Shaw this insatiable capitalist is certainly no villain. If he lacks some of the softer affections, he has none of the small, mean, petty vices. Lady Britomart may snub him, but he grudges no generous support. And he is pleased to provide his workers with comforts, once his own wealth has been assured.

He is selfish, Shaw would probably admit. But the playwright also seemed certain that whatever dangers might be present would be largely counteracted by such an individual's high intelligence. As Undershaft points out, poverty not only blights those immediately affected but the whole society. So if the intelligent individual wants to feel happy and secure himself, he will, as a matter of course, try to make things as pleasant for others as possible. Undershaft would much prefer, thus, to be "Dandy Andy" to his employees than a feared and hated brute.

Finally, he is admired by Shaw because he lives up to his potential, thus cooperating with the "Life-Force" that seeks the raising of the race to ever higher levels. He does not ask for love. He wants only to be kept on his mettle, so that he may go on achieving. In saving his workers from poverty, in bringing Barbara in to elevate their spirits, in developing new inventions, even in contributing to save the Army shelter, he is contributing to human progress. And that to Shaw is the crucial test of greatness.

## ADOLPHUS CUSINS

Although the characterization is allegedly based on the personality of Shaw's friend, Gilbert Murray, and although

Cusins now and then cites Euripides, Barbara's fiance in many ways resembles Undershaft, the superman he will succeed.

First of all, Cusins has a lively, active mind. Even his sardonic quips can be quite subtle, and he misses little that goes on. He can spot the Machiavellian scheming of Undershaft because he himself is astute. He has, of course, deceived Barbara somewhat as to his Army conversion and satisfied his own scruples by means of hair-splitting distinctions.

In addition, he is not at all slow about realizing his ambitions. He may have been surprised to find out that Barbara was rich, but he went right on courting her. And now let someone drop a hint about the Undershaft foundling requirement, and he is busy thinking up ways and means of securing the plum for himself.

Unlike the fully matured Shavian hero, he is still partially the romantic. He is terribly alarmed at the thought of losing Barbara, although the more restrained Undershaft assures him that there is really little difference between one young and man and the next. Nevertheless, he proves that he has leadership potential, in the sense preferred by Shaw, when he makes his crucial decision without consulting her.

Two other weaknesses, however, are apparent. He still does not have any icy control of his nerves. He still gets dangerously excited. And again, no ideal Shavian figure would ever be caught drinking too much, although it is significant that even when allowing himself to be given too much wine, Cusins avoids making any hasty commitment.

Finally, there is that altruistic streak present in most of Shaw's admired figures. Cusins is a little vague as to just how he plans to use the vast munitions works to help the common people and end wars, but he is a man of some vision and is therefore likely to do something constructive. His bargaining with Undershaft indicates that he will not neglect any intelligent self-interest. Chances are that he will get all that he deserves and quite a bit more. But there is nothing small or petty about his dreams. He too, like Barbara and her father, contemplates the future with a great eagerness to achieve.

## BARBARA UNDERSHAFT

Unlike her brother and her sister, Barbara has left the secure confines of her Wilton Crescent home and gone forth to help humanity. Vivacious and energetic, she reveals traits surprisingly similar to those of the other two characters held up for approval.

She, too, is intelligent. She may make some youthful errors. She is slow in spotting the deceptions of both Cusins and the spurious converts. And it would seem that she does underestimate her own father. What an unlikely prospect for a Salvation Army conversion! Yet in other ways she is remarkably astute. She will not let Walker cancel out one wrong by committing another. She sees immediately the implications of the Army's acceptance of the check. And subsequently she can appreciate the merits of her father's contentions.

Secondly, she is a forceful individual with a strong will. Even the formidable Lady Britomart is comically afraid of her. And the great Undershaft visibly flinches when she advances bitterly to pin her emblem on his coat. She is not afraid of the ruffian Walker, who has just brutally struck two women. And she is relentless in her efforts to force him to acknowledge his need for salvation. Furthermore, she has no use for weakness in others. Had Cusins feared to accept her father's offer, she informs him, she would have married whatever daring individual had taken up the challenge.

Finally, she, too, is someone with vision. As a young woman engaged to marry, she might be expected to be concerned about establishing her home. But she flatly assures Cusins that the mere delights of the fireside will never satisfy her. And she tells her father that if necessary she would have given up Cusins to the slaughter rather than lose Walker's soul. It may not be altogether apparent exactly what she intends to do to raise the spirits of her father's well-fed, uppish workers. But she is prepared to devote herself, as she did in the past, to furthering the progress of her people. And this qualifies her as a Shavian heroine.

## BILL WALKER

In quite a few Shaw plays, there are independent lower-class characters who seem to be credited with unusual potential. Bill Walker is an outspoken Cockney with none of the fawning servility that renders unappealing those accepting the shelter's dole.

In striking Jenny, Bill acts with uncontrolled anger, aggravated by drinking. He is not wholly insensitive, however, and at least actively seeks some solution for his problem. He also has no debilitating awe of the gentry, although realistically aware of their police power, and can argue quite boldly with an Earl's granddaughter.

Walker is not one to cherish romantic illusions. He knows at once that Todger can down him and also recognizes Barbara's superior qualities. Yet he values highly his own freedom and is quick to seize upon the weaknesses of the Army's position. At the same time, he is not wholly ungenerous. His bribe offer was, for him, munificent. And his jaunty farewell to the discouraged Barbara is not wholly unsympathetic. Bill is by no means the fully developed hero. But he does have possibilities.

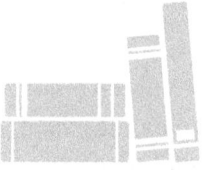

# MAJOR BARBARA

## ESSAY QUESTIONS AND ANSWERS

Question: Select and discuss briefly three important **themes** in Shaw's *Major Barbara*.

Answer: First of all there is the idea that poverty is the worst of crimes. Shaw reveals some of the evils spawned by want in his scenes at the West Ham shelter. Shirley is weak and tottering from starvation, and the others are ill-fed and ill-clothed. In addition, being wholly dependent upon others, the poor become mean and hypocritical, losing all personal dignity as they turn into servile liars. In Undershaft's speeches, Shaw also suggests that the diseases they suffer can spread to the wealthy and that the latter are forced to maintain police forces and inflict cruel penalties in order to preserve their privileged status. By contrast, the activities of professional criminals are not nearly so harmful. Poverty is a blight that affects all social levels.

The second theory is that an awakened conscience is the best deterrent against the repetition of offenses. Shaw objects to harsh legal penalties, believing that one crime does not excuse another act of cruelty. In addition he does not want any culprit to think he can "pay" for his offense, either by sentence or by voluntary offering, because he may then feel free to start anew. For this reason, Shaw also dislikes the Christian dogma of atonement through the merits of Christ, the Redeemer; for again he feels that the evil-doer, once justified, may sin again. His solution, as demonstrated by Barbara, is to convince the guilty party that his act is irrevocable and make him feel such remorse that he will never want to experience again such spiritual discomfort.

The third point stressed is the role of wealth and power. Undershaft laughs scornfully at Stephen's assumption that governments are run independently. He claims that wealthy capitalists, such as he, declare the wars, dictate the policies of the press, and tell political leaders how to proceed. Later, Barbara is convinced that neither the Army nor any other vital work can advance without the financial support of such as Bodger, the whiskey manufacturer, and her father, who makes munitions. To reject them is to turn one's back on life. And her fiance finally decides that he must take his place in the Undershaft business to obtain the wealth and influence he needs to elevate the common people. Throughout the play, Shaw emphasizes again and again the paramount role of money in assuring the good life for all.

Question: Undershaft is an unscrupulous munitions magnate, often described in words suggesting the infernal or diabolical. To what extent is he then Shaw's hero?

Answer: Shaw vigorously denied that he had taken over the philosopher Nietzsche's cult of the Superman. But he seems to have great admiration for a certain type of exceptional individual, well represented by Undershaft.

For one thing, the armaments king is highly intelligent. He has an alert, supple mind and uses it constantly to advantage.

Secondly, he has definite goals and pursues them with single-minded purpose. Undershaft wanted to avoid poverty and worked and fought his way to the summit of a great industrial organization. He decides to win over Barbara and lets nothing stand in his way.

Thirdly, his nature is such that he is not the prey of the softer emotions of lesser men. His wife might plead before and plead now, but he is not going to name Stephen his successor. And again no sentimental fondness for his daughter will induce him to let her continue her Army service undisturbed.

Fourthly, he is no "romantic," but a "realist." He takes into account the harsh and ugly facts of life and acts accordingly. And finally in some sense he is a "mystic." He has a more comprehensive vision than other men and realizes that in carrying out his own bold designs, he is achieving a high level of human development, thus cooperating with the universal and mysterious "Life-Force."

Question: Despite its obvious intellectual content, *Major Barbara* is usually considered one of Shaw's comedies. Does the dramatist use any standard comic devices in this play?

Answer: Although the playwright does seem most interested in the theories he is putting forth about the ills of society, he often relieves tensions with amusing incidents such as could appear in much less cerebral works.

First of all, there are certain characters who resemble others who often appear in standard pieces. There is, for instance, the assertive Lady Britomart, typical of many "pouter pigeon dowagers." Then there is Lomax, the silly young upper-class dandy, who always makes the wrong or vapid comment. And then there is Stephen, the stiffly correct nonentity who "knows nothing and ... thinks he knows everything."

There are also comic situations. Having been warned that Rummy and Snobby are liars, it is amusing to watch them impose upon the lasses. Bill's encounter with Todger Fairmile sounds quite funny, and Lomax's casual handling of matches in the munitions shed has its own note of grim hilarity.

There are, however, still other elements worth noting briefly. The very use of dialect in the West Ham scenes is one. Some of Walker's Cockney terms are amusingly pungent. There are also subtler verbal jokes, as when Undershaft is clearly and deliberately ambiguous. And finally there is the high comedy of cross purpose skillfully handled in the scene in which the Army is "bought."

Question: In the course of his plays, Shaw represents certain of his characters as cooperating with the "Life-Force," that is, fulfilling the destiny for which they were intended. Cite examples of this in *Major Barbara*.

Answer: The initial example of this is Lady Britomart, in her efforts to secure Stephen's inheritance. According to the theory, the ordinary woman finds her life work in continuing the race by having children. She thus wants to find a good husband for herself who will steadily provide for her and her young. Naturally, she opposes any suggestion of originality or unconventionality since geniuses, being unappreciated, are often poor providers. She thus continues the race but does little to raise it to a higher level. Lady Britomart has tried all along to get Andrew Undershaft to name their son as his heir. Since Stephen is incompetent, such a decision will halt whatever progress the superior Andrew has achieved. But Lady Britomart must try to bring this about.

And Undershaft, as a man of exceptional talent, must in turn cooperate with the life force by opposing her attempts to ruin his long-range plans.

Barbara in this play seems closer to the theoretical male who furthers progress rather than the woman who prepares the next generation. She is in some way through her ministrations helping to educate the minds and thus enfranchise the poor.

Question: In *Major Barbara* Shaw's heroine becomes disillusioned and gives up her work at the West Ham shelter. Is Shaw's treatment of the Salvation Army in the play completely hostile?

Answer: If Shaw's statements in his preface are accurate, many who saw the play when it first opened had conflicting views as to his attitude. Some felt that in having the Army accept the donations from Bodger and Undershaft he was castigating the group for crass materialism. Others wondered why his heroine should object so to what was obviously a sensible and justifiable expedient.

Actually, Shaw's attitude seems to be complex. On the one hand, he likes a great deal about the Army. In contrast to some other religious denominations, he finds their spirit joyous and positive. And as a devotee of music, he likes their lively bands and stirring march music. In addition, he approves of their fighting spirit. They selflessly and steadily oppose evils with militant zeal, and their motto is "Blood and Fire." On the whole, his Salvation Army workers are attractive enough, and he does not seem to condemn outright the taking of the donation. This is realistic. What else could they do?

He does, however, have certain objections. He dislikes their emphasis upon emotional confessions, because he thinks that these encourage born liars like Snobby and Rummy. He also feels that there may be a certain morbid interest on the part of the spectators rather than any true religious feelings. He resents, too, whatever the Army does to encourage a spirit of tame acceptance and resignation. He would rather have the poor fight for their rights than be humbly grateful for a bit of bread and treacle. Finally, one suspects that he agrees with Lomax that there is a certain amount of "tosh" about its other teachings. Shaw wants very little emphasis upon the life hereafter, bribe or no bribe.

In general, then, he does not condemn the Army. It does a certain amount of good in feeding the starving and encouraging the drink-sodden and abandoned to mend their ways and behave with human dignity. Mog washed her red hair and began to know new joy. Nevertheless, he reserves for his Barbara a higher destiny. She must appreciate, as he does, the limitations of the Army's work among the poor, and go on to something better. Once having been forced to see the light, she must devote herself to the well-fed and the quarrelsome and bring them to loftier and holier thoughts, recognizing the starved souls in full bodies. She will be, by inference, a somewhat unorthodox Salvation Army Major in the future, but she will retain the fervor and the cheerfulness and the positive approach that Shaw so thoroughly commends.

Question: A great deal of attention is paid to Bill Walker in the play. What dramatic and other purposes does the character serve?

Answer: First of all, Walker sets up the whole discussion of conscience and atonement. Bill, outraged by the desertion of this girl, Mog, a Salvation Army convert, comes to the shelter demanding that she be surrendered to him for a beating. Not being instinctively brutal, he has nerved himself with gin. When Mog is not produced, he strikes hard a young Salvationist lass, Jenny Hill, and an old convert Rummy Mitc ens.

By ably impressing him with the monstrous nature of his deed, Barbara makes him feel remorseful. To ease his conscience, he then attempts to get for himself a retributory beating from a convert wrestler. When this fails, he offers as fine a pound he has painfully saved. Barbara refuses all "bribes." He must mourn his deed, regard it as irrevocable, and accepting "Salvation," amend his life. When, however, the Army takes the large "conscience" donation from Bodger, Bill cynically refuses to bow.

On the whole, Bill is the argumentative, cocky, far from servile poor man that Shaw prefers to the whining sycophants. He is also a comic figure, as he tells of being knelt on and prayed over by Todger, or airily bids Barbara, "Sao Long, Judy." Finally, he represents Barbara's principal grudge against her highhanded father who interrupted the "conversion," as well as Undershaft's prime theoretical example of the civilizing benefits of high wages.

Question: Indicate several functions of the minor characters in *Major Barbara*.

Answer: The major figures should probably be considered to include Undershaft, Barbara, Cusins, and, perhaps, Bill Walker. The others in the Undershaft and Army circles are used for **exposition**, **satire**, and humorous relief from tension.

The **exposition** function is apparent in the very first scene as Lady Britomart informs Stephen about the break with his father, the Undershaft tradition of choosing foundlings as heirs, and the general financial situation of the girls and their fiances. Snobby and Rummy tell us later something about how the shelter operates, and Stephen and Sarah give some account of the wonders of Perivale St. Andrews.

Secondly, they may be used as satiric representations of a type of behavior of which Shaw disapproves. Lomax. for instance, is a vain and silly young man. Rummy and Snobby illustrate how the poor can be induced to turn into servile hypocrites. And Stephen is a lamentable example of all that Shaw thinks wrong in contemporary education.

Finally, they add refreshing comic touches. Lady Britomart is an amusingly overbearing dowager, and the liars at the shelter are droll rogues. There is also something inevitably funny about the blundering Lomax, especially when he insists that matches are perfectly safe in a munitions shed.

Question: Not all aspects of *Major Barbara* have been universally lauded. Discuss briefly some that have been regarded critically.

Answer: The earliest attacks seem to have been upon the play's reliance more upon discussion that upon action. As Shaw himself admitted, the third act is largely a debate, and some would prefer that there be more of the conventionally dramatic in the work's development.

Secondly, there have been questions as to the credibility of certain decisions by the characters. Chesterton, for one, was astounded that the clever professor of Greek puts up such a weak case on behalf of his way of life. And not a few have wondered about Barbara's final, rather unexpected decision to transfer her ministry to her father's well-fed workers.

Finally, there have been some serious criticisms of the points of view expressed. For instance, Chesterton, again, challenged the implication that vice is inevitably linked with poverty, virtue with wealth. And others have seen in Undershaft's spirited assertions merely the rationalizations of a cold, selfish individual. Still others have been skeptical about Barbara's explanation regarding the "bride of bread," inquiring whether or not the Undershaft wages and other benefits are not also bribes of a sort. This is a stimulating play of ideas, with many controversial opinions. Naturally, some have been vigorously opposed.

Question: Explain why the generally admired Undershaft is called sometimes "mad," or "infernal" or given to Machiavellian schemes.

Answer: Like his heroes, Shaw delights in shocking his hearers with seemingly outrageous notions. Actually, however, some sort of reversal is usually suggested. When Shaw attacks social evils, he is criticizing often institutions or customs that have been reputed falsely in his view to be sane and good. In preaching the opposite he or his spokesmen may appear, from the standpoint of the unenlightened, mad and diabolical. Shaw, in other words, suggests that only by rigorously opposing entrenched theories, when such are causing harm, can progress be achieved. But the narrow-minded will always find reformers "mad" and "vicious."

Question: What does "salvation" mean in *Major Barbara*?

Answer: Actually, it means different things to different characters. Barbara and Mrs. Baines would have their people be saved by accepting the message of the Salvation Army. Undershaft, however, equates salvation with freedom from economic pressures. In general, Shaw would consider the saved individual one who, being relatively free from poverty, could and would devote himself to some great work contributing to the progress of the race. Such a person, cooperating with the Life-Force, achieves the highest dignity possible to man. As for the life hereafter, Shaw leaves the question open. But the stress is on the satisfactions gained from living up to one's potential and elevating one's fellow-men.

www.ingramcontent.com/pod-product-compliance
Lightning Source LLC
LaVergne TN
LVHW011709060526
838200LV00051B/2825